To my husband ...
exciting, knowledgea... ...

With all my love
Joanie

SKIN and SCUBA
DIVING

SKIN and SCUBA DIVING

by George X. Sand

Illustrated with photographs and line drawings

ACTION BOOKS

for today's young adults

A POPULAR MECHANICS PRESS BOOK

Hawthorn Books, Inc., New York and London

All photographs appearing in this book have been photographed at, and are the courtesy of, Florida's Silver Springs.

H-8297

To my delightful wife,
Phyllis,
a faithful buddy always at hand.

ACKNOWLEDGMENTS

The author wishes to thank long-time diving friends Wm. B. Ray and Ricou Browning, both of Ocala, Florida, for encouraging the writing of this book and for the latter's Foreword. Bill Ray has been SCUBA diving since the first risky lungs were introduced; Ricou, co-author of the hit film "Flipper" and strong-swimming star of the "Creature of the Black Lagoon" series of movies, has acted in over 100 sequences of the "Sea Hunt" TV productions, and will shortly be directing technically a new underwater TV series.

On the nation's opposite coast, Californians Zale Perry, who holds the women's world record for deep diving, and famed movieland underwater cameraman Lamar Boren ("The Old Man and the Sea" and similar successes) likewise proved cooperative and understanding.

Between these two geographical extremes, other diving enthusiasts like Bud and Patsie Boyett, Newton and Dot Perry, pioneer SCUBA-man Glen Galvin, Jack McEarchern, veteran diving photographer Bruce Mozert, and others not mentioned by name in the text likewise rose up to help unselfishly, motivated by the dedicated skin diver's common love for a fine sport and his willingness to share it with others.

Finally, I wish to thank the management at Silver Springs, Florida, for permitting their SCUBAmaids and SCUBAmen to pose so helpfully and patiently in their Voit diving outfits while we made the pictures that illustrate the various procedures described in the book.

G. X. S.

Boca Raton, Florida
March 1, 1964

Foreword

The author is a world traveler and adventurer, and a perfectionist always. This last habit—of much importance to the would-be skin diver—will be found manifesting itself from the first to the last pages of this excellent book. I can unhesitatingly recommend this text as a most helpful one for those interested in learning the fine sport of skin diving.

I have known George X. Sand for the past two decades and several times have assisted this veteran newspaperman and magazine journalist complete his literary assignments. I and other outdoor-minded sportsmen have long admired his clear and carefully researched writing. There is no place for guesswork and confusion in skin and SCUBA diving, and a conscientious reading of this book by the beginner will assure him of success as he follows its recommendations step by step under the guidance of a qualified instructor.

Skin and SCUBA diving are fascinating hobbies. Unfortunately, many persons have been discouraged at the outset by the erroneous belief diving calls for exceptional intelligence, unusual physical stamina, or other outstanding attributes. One such popular misconception specifies that one must be in a certain age bracket to dive safely. The truth is that both young and old alike are today gleefully experiencing the delights of discovering what lies beneath the water's surface. They sought competent instruction at the outset. Another misconception is that everyday skin diving is a very expensive sport. The author brings out that this is not necessarily so. In fact, he includes "how to" projects showing you how to make several items of your own equipment.

Skin diving is regarded by many to be one of the fastest-growing sports in America. Recognizing this public demand, the government has created two underwater national parks; one in the

Florida Keys, the other in the Virgin Islands. You owe it to yourself, young or old, male or female, to at least acquaint yourself with this popular form of recreation. For it might well develop into the happy, healthful relaxation that is daily recharging the emotional batteries of thousands of other worried, work-worn Americans.

Ricou Browning
Ocala, Florida
March 20, 1964

Contents

SKIN and SCUBA
DIVING

Scene from an underwater movie being filmed at Silver Springs

1. So You Want to Dive?

Man is a seeker by nature. Almost two thousand years ago when skin-clad shepherds thoughtfully contemplated the stars from darkened hillsides, they felt the same compelling urge to explore which recently sent spacesuit-clad astronauts blasting heavenward from flaming pads at Cape Kennedy.

Before he tackled outer space, man conquered the earth's frontiers one by one: the oceans, the jungles, the air. The vague, shimmering world beneath the water's surface was the last to give way before him. As recently as a decade or two ago, man could only wish he had the ability to explore at will the unseen vistas of ocean, river, or lake.

What awaited him there? Would subterranean caverns yield the remains of animals and reptiles hidden since before the dawn of civilization? Would the explorer stumble upon something valuable that had eluded grasping hands to come to rest on the bottom, lying unclaimed until he chanced by? It might even be lost treasure. Only a small portion of the world's sunken wealth has been recovered. It is reliably estimated that nearly a half *billion* dollars in gold and silver waits beneath the surface somewhere off Florida's sun-washed beaches alone, much of it pirate loot.

The perfection of SCUBA (self-contained underwater breathing apparatus) during World War II provided the answers to these and other questions—answers which you can make as limitless as your own imagination. Picture yourself planing downward gracefully in a long, effortless glide, near weightless at neutral buoyancy, into an iridescent fantasy world of clinking, current-kissed shells; strange emerald forests of sensuously undulating marine growths; schools of brilliantly hued fish that sometimes surround you in

Only a small portion of the world's sunken wealth has been recovered.

living tiers, only inches away and completely unafraid as they accept you as one of their own kind.

Wouldn't it be exciting just to wander aimlessly about this last known frontier on earth? It's not only possible, but within the reach of anyone who wants to try. Simple diving gear costs no more today than other sports equipment. Even once-expensive underwater camera equipment is now available at nominal cost to record the wonders of this soft, silent world.

Here in this challenging new environment wait shadowy, mysterious grottoes; brilliantly lighted bottom fissures, some meandering across the bottom like miniature Grand Canyons; patches of the whitest sand, softly lighted in the moonbeams of the deep, silhouette a disturbed lobster scuttling to safety, swimming backward in characteristic fashion, or a choice fish gliding unsuspecting into range of your speargun. There are unusual rock, shell and marine growth specimens to be collected or photographed, the dim outline of a sunken vessel to be explored, or an outboard motor or other equipment fallen overboard to be recovered.

You will discover—as have some six million other American hobbyists who today happily indulge themselves in this fast-growing sport—that such pleasures can be enjoyed easily and safely with modern SCUBA. First, however, it is vitally important that you prove your physical and mental fitness for such free diving, following this with several hours of qualified instruction (actual time will vary with the individual). This book will help you accomplish this basic education with a minimum of difficulty and expense.

After you have become proficent as a SCUBA diver, you may wish to perform a worthwhile civic duty by making your services available in times of emergency. Perhaps police need assistance in recovering a criminal's weapon suspected of being thrown from a dock. Or maybe trapped coal miners await rescue beyond an accidentally flooded shaft.

In such cases, SCUBA diving, a satisfying sport in itself, becomes a useful and sometimes heroic adventure.

Such willingness to engage in underwater search and recovery can also provide a tidy financial return from your hobby. You will find persons happy to pay you a reasonable fee for assistance

A wreck being explored by SCUBA divers.

in finding and raising sunken small boats, for recovery of lost propellers, fishing tackle and similar items which a careless public is forever losing overboard, and for inspecting damaged boat hulls, docks and what not.

The author knows twin brothers, John and Charles Noyes of Fort Lauderdale, Florida, who launched such a recovery business quite profitably as teenagers. The boys distributed business cards which described them as "The Sea-Triever Twins" and they enjoyed a brisk business recovering underwater objects ranging from boat anchors to watches, rings, and false teeth.

2. Selecting Your Equipment

With few exceptions, today's splashing army of sport divers are either skin divers, breathing through a snorkel tube while swimming at the surface (holding the breath when submerging), or SCUBA divers depending upon a supply of compressed air while swimming below the surface. Stick to these two proven methods and you can enjoy many happy hours of safe fun and exploration. Experimenting with such specialized diving devices as "hard hat" rigs which require the diver's helmet be fed by air hose from a compressor at the surface, or underwater vehicles, oxygen rebreather lungs, and so on, could quickly put you in real trouble. Above all, do not try to save a few dollars by depending upon a homemade SCUBA outfit.

Dependable basic skin diving equipment can be purchased for twenty dollars or less. Since you *must* master this simplest of the two forms of sport diving before turning to SCUBA, let's consider its equipment first.

All you need is a face mask, snorkel tube, swim fins, and safety float. Supplementary items like weight belt, knife, protective suit, spear gun, underwater camera and so on can be purchased later as your interests and skills develop.

A face mask is necessary because water blurs the submerged human vision. However, if we provide air space between the eye and the pressing water, i.e., behind a sheet of protective glass, the eye can blink and function normally. Then we can see objects clearly for considerable distances, depending upon water clarity and surface light conditions, although such objects will be magnified between one-quarter and one-third in size.

Select a sturdy name-brand mask with an untinted shatter-proof glass plate (plastic will scratch), oval or circular in shape. The

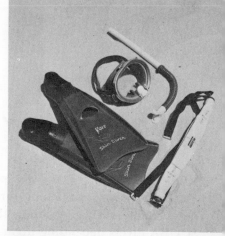

Basic skin diving equipment.

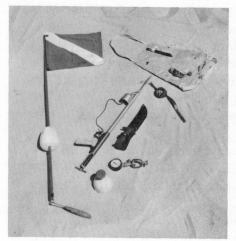

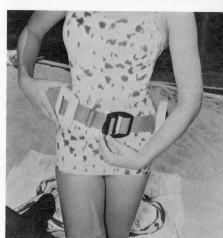

Supplementary equipment can be purchased later.

glass plate should be held securely in place by a rustproof metal rim. Make sure the head strap is strong and adjustable.

It is most important that the mask fits the contour of your face properly to form a watertight union. It should be impossible for air to enter at the edges of the mask when it is in position. Check this in the sporting goods store with your head held level as you look straight ahead, using both hands instead of the headstrap to hold the mask in normal position over your eyes and nose. Inhale

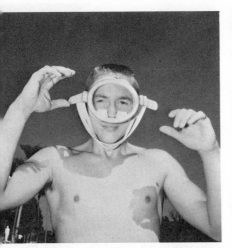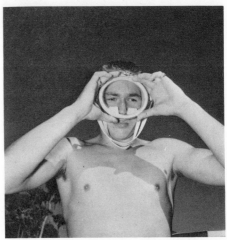

It is most important that the mask fits the contour of your face.

through the nose, simultaneously removing the hands. The vacuum inside the face plate should hold it snugly against your face as long as you attempt to inhale.

Some masks offer such extra features as a small, built-in, one-way exhaust valve and externally operated depth-equalizing, nose pinching, levers at the bottom to make it easier for you to clear the mask underwater, should it flood for some reason, or to "pop" your ears to compensate for changing depth pressures. (Chapter Three will explain these and other important underwater procedures in detail.)

Don't try to use goggles for diving. Since they don't cover the nose, you can't equalize pressures and the glass plates may be forced against your eyes. Forget ear plugs, too. Water pressure may force them inward, endangering your eardrums.

Swim fins make it much easier to propel yourself underwater, thereby increasing your travel range and equipment-carrying capacity. Like masks, they are available in a variety of shapes, sizes, and colors. Most experienced divers prefer the style of flippers with enclosed heel and toes since it protects the feet from sand, coral, and obstructions.

The fins should be carefully chosen to fit the individual. What may be just right for one man may prove just wrong for another.

Mask with external nose pinchers.

Fins should be carefully chosen to fit the individual.

It is best to start with a fin that is relatively flexible for easy swimming. As your legs grow accustomed to these swimming aids, you can graduate to stiffer, faster fins.

Flippers that are too large for your feet will chafe, and may even come off and be lost, especially if they are not the floating type. Too tight a fit can cause trouble, too. I recall a good-natured Miami man who used to join our skin diving group as we explored the Florida Keys reefs. A little fellow whose feet had once been injured in an auto accident, he had difficulty buying fins that would stay on. He was constantly striving for a tighter fit, although we warned him against it.

Late one balmy afternoon as we swam back through the red sunset to our diving boat anchored over a large and colorful ocean reef, we suddenly realized that our diminutive companion was no longer with us. He'd been bringing up the rear, and now we scanned the water uneasily for a sign of him. Finally we began a hurried search.

We found him far downtide, floating on his back, unable to swim, his face pinched with pain. "Boy, am I ever glad to see you guys!" he gasped as we pulled him awkwardly aboard. "My legs—they're killing me!" He had foot cramps so badly he couldn't stand. His too-tight fins had choked off his circulation.

Here's a quick test you can make to see if fins fit properly: wet both feet flippers; if the fin slides into position easily, without being too loose, you have the right size.

The snorkel is a hollow J-shaped tube, usually plastic, about fifteen inches long. It permits you to breathe while swimming face down on the surface. Your lips form a watertight seal over a rubber mouthpiece as you bite down upon it; the other end of the tube remains out of water. To avoid gum irritation, the mouthpiece should fit comfortably, and the tube should be flexible enough to absorb contact jar if it strikes a floating obstacle.

When the snorkeler wants to dive, he inhales through the tube, then holds his breath while submerged like any swimmer. Upon surfacing it is not necessary for him to lift his head. He simply exhales the stale air sharply through the snorkel, clearing it for the next breath.

The snorkel barrel is maintained at the best angle for this operation by securing the tube under the headstrap of your face mask. Strap tension will hold it in place—don't fasten the two together or a snorkel snag can pull off your mask.

Some masks provide single and double snorkel tubes that are built into the rubber at the proper angle. Some snorkels have valves which are intended to close off entering water automatically when you submerge. Most seasoned skin divers avoid these last,

The snorkel permits you to breathe while swimming face downward.

Swimmer exhaling through snorkel.

primarily because they are not necessary, but also because they often leak and can catch in weeds.

Safety floats come in both belt and packet types. Vest types are preferred because they'll float you head-up. Inflated by mouth or built-in carbon dioxide cartridge, the compact units can save your life if you suddenly develop a cramp or find yourself ex-

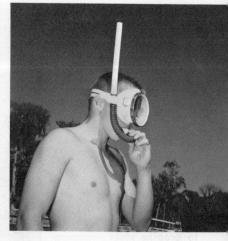

Clearing snorkel after resurfacing.   Correct position of snorkel on head.

hausted. The ideal float works with *both* mouth and CO_2 cartridge inflation. This permits saving the cartridge for a real emergency when you may have no breath left. For instance, after a pleasure-filled afternoon of diving, the shore may prove farther away than you realized. To rest, you need only inflate your body float.

Action of safety float.

SCUBA equipment, to be purchased only after you have mastered basic skin diving, consists of compressed air tank(s) with valve assembly, single or double hose regulator with mouthpiece, and a backpack or strap harness assembly to fasten this equipment securely to your body. A weight belt may prove necessary for you to stay down. This depends upon whether you want positive or negative buoyancy; weights aren't necessary for many divers in fresh water. Supplementary items will include a knife; wrist-type depth gauge, preferably with compass; floating diver's flag to warn boats of your presence (whirling propellers can maim—even kill!); a surface float to transport equipment and specimens and make swimming easier (often the short diver's flag standard is fastened directly to this float); decompression chart; protective suit; spear gun and camera or other equipment as needed.

The compressed air tanks come in various sizes, including 38, 50 and 71.2 cubic foot capacity. The size you select will depend upon how long you wish to remain submerged and what is most comfortable for you. Two 38's, for example, will provide more air than a single big bottle and are considered easier to use by many divers, especially women.

Full SCUBA gear with accessories.

Pure filtered air is compressed inside the tank(s) at pressures of about 2250 pounds per square inch. At average temperature, this represents about an hour of air supply for a diver using a 70 cubic foot tank near the surface, providing he's had some SCUBA breathing experience and does not exert himself unusually. Under normal conditions you will require about one cubic foot of air per minute.

Your lungs are accustomed to functioning at an air pressure of one atmosphere (14.7 pounds per square inch) at sea level. Obviously, therefore, it would prove disastrous to try to breathe compressed air directly from the tank(s) at 2,250 p.s.i. A regulating device is necessary to reduce this high air pressure to a value suitable for your lungs to handle.

This would be easy to do were it not for the fact that a SCUBA diver's lungs will require compressed air at different pressures for different depths. Let's assume you don your SCUBA gear and slip into the water at sea level. Here your body is surrounded by a pressure of 14.7 p.s.i. This external pressure against your chest will call for a given effort to expand your rib cage outward against the pressure, thereby providing space for air to enter your collapsible lung areas. As we've stated, your lungs are used to functioning normally at sea level, and you experience no breathing problem.

But now let's dive. To the normal atmospheric pressure is now added a second pressure upon your body and lungs: the constantly increasing pressure, i.e., weight, of the water as you go deeper. At a depth of thirty-three feet, we find a combined atmospheric and water pressure of 29.4 p.s.i., twice that at the surface, pressing inward upon your chest, making it difficult to breathe unless we somehow increase the pressure of the air entering your lungs. Your body's solid and liquid areas, unlike the lungs, aren't nearly so compressible and hence are not so subject to these water pressure effects.

In other words, at a depth of thirty-three feet and a combined pressure of two atmospheres, your body requires compressed air at twice the surface pressure. Hence your air supply will last only half as long at this depth for the same amount of exertion. Should you descend to sixty-six feet, your body will become subject to an additional atmosphere of pressure, a total of three, or 44.1 p.s.i.,

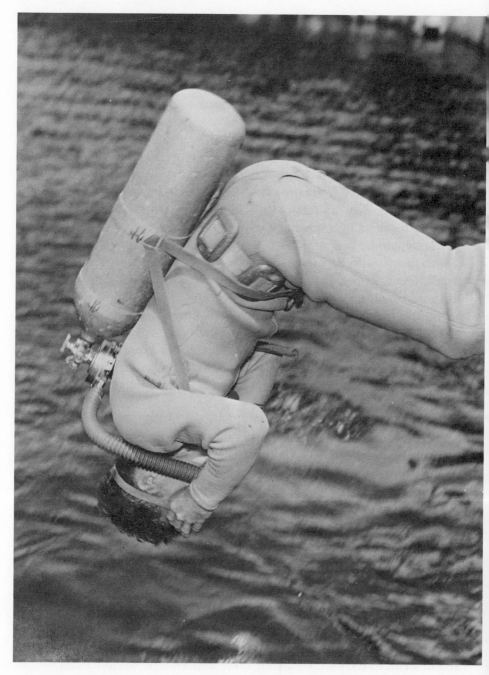

"But now, let's dive."

and your compressed air supply can be expected to last about one-third the time it would had you remained near the surface.

It becomes evident, therefore, that the regulating device between the tank and the diver's lungs must perform a double function. First, it must reduce the tank pressure to lung pressure. Second, the regulator must constantly supply air to the lungs at a pressure which will match, or equalize the effects of, the combined and varying air and water pressures upon the diver's body as he descends and returns to the surface.

One such control is the popular open-circuit demand type SCUBA regulator in wide use today. Briefly, it works like this: the diaphragm in the regulator air chamber is acted upon on one side by compressed air pressure from the tank(s) and on the opposite side by opposing pressure from the water in which the diver is swimming. As the diaphragm moves in one direction or the other, depending upon which of these two pressures proves the greater at the moment, it opens or closes a valve which limits the amount of air entering the regular chamber from the tank, and, subsequently, the diver's lungs. Hence the pressure of the compressed air passing through the regulator into the diver's lungs is automatically made equal to the pressure of the water at whatever depth it may be operating. This provides constant normal breathing pressure.

Exhaled air is passed through a non-return valve in the opposite side of the diver's mouthpiece, through the second, or exhaust, hose and out into the surrounding water through another non-return valve in the regulator.

Mention a diver's knife to the average person and he envisions a shark fight. Nonsense. The average blade isn't long enough to reach a shark's vitals—even if you were strong enough to drive it through the fish's tough hide. Depend instead upon your sheath knife for cutting away entangling underwater obstructions, prying loose submerged objects, removing and cleaning speared fish, and so on.

Select a rustproof blade of good steel and keep it sharp. The author prefers a Randall stainless steel knife, worn at belt, thigh, or calf and secured against loss by a keeper thong. Some divers prefer a floating knife with handle of buoyant material; most do not.

Your weight belt *must* incorporate a quick-release buckle, or fold-back belt knot if a D-ring is used instead, that can be easily operated by one hand should an emergency demand that you ditch your equipment and rise to the surface. The belt should be impervious to water and should permit easy addition and removal of individual weights since the amount of equipment you carry, like the clothing you wear, will change your buoyancy. A protective suit, for example, is quite buoyant and will call for extra weights.

Before you can weight yourself properly, you must know beforehand what you intend to accomplish underwater. If you expect to work on the bottom, extra weights may be necessary. If you wish to rise slowly surfaceward when you stop swimming (positive buoyancy), or vice versa, weights can be adjusted to the point where you ascend or descend each time you draw in or exhale a breath.

Your surface float can be a hollow paddleboard with cut-out viewing port forward for your face mask as you stretch prone and kick along. Or it can be a sturdy inflated surfmat. Even an inflated innertube will do nicely, provided it is in good condition. It is common practice to attach a diver's flag to an innertube float anchored to the bottom, to warn boatmen you are operating in the area. Design of the standard diver's flag will be discussed in the next chapter. The use of decompression tables and such specialized accessory items as spear guns and cameras will likewise be treated in detail in subsequent chapters.

Just as with any other major sport, there are many accessory items on the market to entrance the devotees of SCUBA. Some of these goodies that crop up year after year prove to be of temporary value, it is true, but most serve a definite purpose in advancing enjoyment of the sport.

The built-in one-way water exhaust valve which most of the better face masks offer today, for example, does provide a faster and easier way to purge water from a mask when it floods. This small flutter valve, about the size of a quarter, is usually built right into the glass face plate. However, one mask features a special diaphragm in this position which will make possible short-range underwater speech with other divers.

Today's face plates vary widely in design. Some black goggle-

Instructor demonstrating quick-release buckle.

like masks are apt to give you the appearance of a glaring man from Mars, while others resemble wrap-around windshields, said to afford 180-degree vision. To better insure a leakproof face seal, one features a double instead of single rubber feather-edge. And if you are a SCUBA man who must wear glasses, one diving optician advertises that he will provide a pair of oversize wide-angle lenses ground to your prescription and custom fitted to the inside of your mask for twenty-five dollars or less.

The latest mouthpieces are easy to clear when they become flooded. One combination mouthpiece-regulator unit has been made so compact it is worn before the face, below the nose, and boasts a built-in purge button. Twin exhaust ports channel the bubbles away from your face, preventing interference with your vision. The regulator is designed so that reducing tank pressure, as the air is used up, does not call for increased breathing effort. And some current mouthpieces provide a chin rest to reduce jaw fatigue and possible cramps during long dives.

One weight belt now on the market is designed to expand and contract about your waist without strain as you breathe. Another provides only a single pouch on the belt which holds ten removable one-pound discs.

For less than twenty dollars, you can equip yourself with a sealed-beam battery-operated underwater light. Guaranteed for depths to two hundred feet, it will float to the surface should you accidentally "drop" it.

If you have a bit more to spend, two hundred dollars will buy a portable bottom dredge with four-inch suction intake, powered by a lightweight four-cycle gasoline engine-compressor. You can set the little power plant up on shore or on a boat, connected by hose to the hand-held "sniffer" which you work along the bottom like a vacuum cleaner. When you return to the surface, you remove the unit's "riffle box" to see what—if anything—you've dredged up. Another underwater prospector's tool is claimed to develop tremendous suction "for pulling nuggets out of narrow crevices" as continuous automatic panning ejects the unwanted sand and gravel.

Perhaps you would like to present a self-winding, waterproof wristwatch to your favorite diver. These come from one hundred dollars up and are pressure tested to depths in excess of six hundred feet. They offer such built-in innovations as telemeter and tachymeter in addition to the usual stop watch with extra-bright, glowing numerals for easy reading in the dark depths. One watch has an adjustable outer rim which warns when your safe diving time is up for any preselected depth. And you can purchase a portable pressure gauge, for attachment to tank valve or regulator, which will tell at a glance how much air remains in your cylinder at any time during a dive.

A 55-pound portable compressor unit is designed for the convenience of the traveling diver who is not sure he can purchase air to refill his bottle away from home.

The latest "wet suits" are being made with a combination neoprene and nylon lining. You don't need talcum powder or grease to put them on easily, wet or dry.

A new "corrosion and impact-proof" tank harness, contoured to fit the user's back, offers an attached handle for carrying it and its two 50-cubic-foot short tanks. The twin bottles provide twenty-eight per cent more diving time over the single 71.8-cubic-foot tank and offer no interference when you wish to sit.

Someone has even come up with a waterproof, plastic slide rule that gives "instant, accurate" decompression table readings.

A novel portable diver's rescue kit has appeared, hardly larger than a lunch box. It contains a mouth-to-mouth resuscitator which enables the rescuer to blow through a valved hose and into the victim's lungs via a mask that is fitted over his face. As the rescuer inhales to complete the respiration cycle, exhaled air from the victim's lungs is automatically ejected through an exhaust port.

If you are the type that tires easily, you and your buddy can ride around together underwater at four m.p.h. in your own open-cockpit submarine, or be towed by an electric "torpedo scooter." And you can buy an underwater communications set that will enable you to carry on intercom conversations without moving a swim fin.

You can save yourself money by making your own protective suit for cold water diving. For temperatures not much below 70 degrees Fahrenheit, a wool sweater or other garment may provide sufficient warmth by helping keep the same water against your body. But for prolonged diving in cold water—and it grows colder the deeper one goes—a rubber suit of the wet or dry variety becomes a must.

The dry suit, as the name implies, is substantially watertight. It is made of thin rubber that fits snugly over woolen or insulating underwear. To avoid pressure "squeeze," you must provide for release of the air trapped inside the suit before diving. (One easy way to do this is to hold up one arm, keeping an opening at the wrist, as you walk into the water.) The dry suit has the disadvantage of tearing easily, in which case you immediately lose both insulation and buoyancy.

The more popular foam-rubber wet suit purposely permits some water to enter between it and the body. This water quickly becomes warmed from body heat and serves as insulation against cold. The full suit consists of separate feet, pants, shirt, hood and gloves. Usually only the shirt and pants need be worn, and often the shirt alone will suffice when diving would be uncomfortable otherwise.

The foam rubber comes in a choice of colors and thicknesses, depending upon your insulation need. You simply lay it in sheet form under an available pattern to match your build (a pattern which you buy; or you can try making your own if you prefer). The sheet rubber is then cut out and the pieces fastened together with a rubber contact cement.

Allow the cemented surfaces to dry before holding them together. The contact cement will form a strong bond. Subsequent rips and holes in the suit from later use can be repaired just as easily.

3. How To Use It — Safely

The frightened boy lay in the hospital, nearly drowned. He was alive only because a second SCUBA diver, luckily, happened to swim past within visual range and notice him lying unconscious on the bottom.

The boy's father was furious as he answered the questions of reporters. "I provided my son the best skin diving apparatus you can buy. It even included an instant-inflating body float, supposed to carry him quickly to the surface should anything go wrong. I'm going to demand they outlaw these dangerous diving gadgets to protect the public from them!"

Other citizens in the coastal area took up the indignant cry as they read the newspaper stories. The boy, seventeen, was an excellent swimmer, a high school athlete in top physical condition. The shiny new diving lung *had* to be at fault.

"No, you're wrong," countered a suntanned, veteran SCUBA man as he stood up to accost the angry father at a public meeting. "It's true you bought your son the very best equipment. But you turned him loose without first making certain he knew how to use it. That's like sending him up to pilot his own plane without instruction."

To prove his point, the husky speaker challenged all present to accompany him to the site of the near-disaster on the following day. There, while his audience watched apprehensively, he donned the "faulty" SCUBA equipment and dove repeatedly to the bottom without difficulty.

"The boy simply panicked down there, that's all," the veteran explained as he walked ashore. "Any untrained adult diver could have had the same difficulty. Maybe he accidentally knocked loose his face mask, causing it to flood so he couldn't see. Or an unexpected sneeze may have made him lose his mouthpiece, filling it with water so he thought he could no longer get air."

It's easy to clear a flooded mask or mouthpiece underwater, provided you've practiced beforehand with a qualified instructor. Neglect such training and you leave yourself a wide open target for panic—the worst thing that can happen to a skin diver. Remember this: man was not put on this earth primarily to fly like a bird or swim like a fish. When you decide to invade these new mediums, you must first train and condition yourself. Having done this, the chances are good that you can calmly meet each new situation as it arises, overcoming the problem because you know beforehand what to expect. The experienced airplane pilot, for instance, doesn't jump out of the cockpit should his gas supply fail for some reason; he simply switches to a reserve tank as the SCUBA diver does to a second compressed air tank—or, if necessary, the SCUBA diver breathes temporarily from another diver's tank long enough to regain the surface.

Where can you, a beginner, find a qualified instructor? Ask at your local sporting goods or divers' supply store where you can contact other SCUBA devotees, or, better still, join a club. For a nominal fee, you can join the Underwater Society of America, an organization dedicated to the education and representation of American skin divers.

Meanwhile, let's assume that I am to be your instructor while we go through the standard diver's instruction course, step by step, for the remainder of this chapter.

First, though you may look healthy and appear emotionally stable, we must make sure. There is no point in investing your time and money for SCUBA equipment and training unless your doctor will first confirm your mental and physical fitness for this hobby, using the regular skin diver's medical examination form. Some persons suffer shortcomings which no amount of training can correct. Faulty eustachian tubes or a permanent perforation of an eardrum, for example, will prevent the sinuses and middle ear from adjusting to the changing pressures as the skin diver attempts to "clear" his ears. Also, you should obviously not be a victim of heart, respiratory, or emotional disorders. A person subject to fainting spells, claustrophobia, and similar weaknesses should not venture underwater. And one must, of course, be able to dive and swim reasonably well.

If you pass your physical, we will take face mask, swim fins, body float and snorkel (no compressed air yet!) and proceed to a shallow section of a nearby lake. Note that I said "we." You *never* go skin diving without a companion. *Never.*

First, show me you can swim two hundred yards, any style, without fins or float. An emergency might someday arise where you must get yourself to safety without such aids.

After this I will expect you to demonstrate your ability to tread water for five minutes, thirty seconds of that time with your hands held above the surface. You'll have to swim underwater for thirty feet, retrieve an object in eight feet of water, and tow me—as an "injured" diver—on the surface for seventy-five feet. Sometime you may have to help your buddy or another swimmer.

Next let's turn our attention to the safety float fastened around your waist. Inflate the float as you tread water. Practice floating on it, swimming with it. Never dive without it. And form the habit right now of not counting too heavily on the self-inflating cartridge to work every time, or the little float to save you infallibly from any situation you may get yourself into. Never take chances in the water. Always play it safe.

Someday you may have to tow another diver.

Rub saliva, kelp, soap, glycerine, or any of the prepared de-fogging substances, across the inner glass surface of your face plate and rinse it off. If you don't take this precaution, the glass may fog from temperature differences between its inner and outer surfaces. Put the mask on. Adjust the head strap for a snug fit that won't leak air when you try to inhale through the nose. Take a good breath through the mouth, put your head under, and dive from the surface. How clearly you can see in this soft, new, water-cushioned world!

Clearing face plate with saliva or kelp.

But what's this? The deeper you go the more uncomfortable you may become. The rubber of your mask may seem to be sucking and flattening against your face. Here's why: the water pressure has become greater than the counter-pressure inside your mask. To remedy this face plate "squeeze," exhale gently through the nose until the pressure imbalance and mask discomfort disappear. You will soon find yourself doing this automatically without conscious effort.

Should your ears, maybe even your sinuses, become uncomfortable, more pressure equalizing is in order. Such discomfort is caused when the external pressure against your yielding eardrums becomes greater than the pressure of the air confined inside your head and respiratory passages. Swallow first. If this doesn't correct the situation, hold the nostrils closed and blow gently against the resistance. Caution: don't blow hard or you may damage delicate tissues in the body's air spaces.

When pressure has thus been equalized on both sides of the eardrum, you will feel normal again. A slight "pop" may be felt during the process. This "clearing" the ears must be repeated at intervals as you vary your diving depth. It becomes easier and more automatic as you gain experience.

Some divers prefer to wear a nose clip inside their masks to facilitate this procedure. Others depend upon an indentation

Equalizing pressure by gently blowing nose with nostrils closed.

at the soft rubber underside of their face plate to permit the fingers to grip the nose. Some better masks, as mentioned earlier, have built-in externally-operated nose-pinching levers. If your mask is a simple one, without such conveniences, you can also hold it tightly against the face with both hands, then slide it carefully upward until the bottom seals your nostrils shut.

Don't underestimate the importance of this pressure equaliza-

The instructor showing the student the usefulness of externally operated nose-pinching levers.

tion. Disregard it and it is quite possible to rupture an eardrum while diving *in only ten feet of water.* This painful injury may require several weeks to heal. Should water enter the broken eardrum, you may suffer vertigo and lose all sense of equilibrium while submerged, and even ashore.

Of course, you could simply have removed your mask and held your nose closed with your fingers to blow against the stoppage— just as you might have done had you been climbing a mountain— without the face plate. Many seasoned divers do this when swallowing fails to clear the ears. But removal of your mask like that will, of course, let water reach your face. And, since you haven't been taught yet how to clear such a flooded mask, the

Instructor shows student how to swim with up-and-down "flutter" kick movement from hips.

sudden discomfort and loss of vision could cause you to panic—just as it did the untrained diver described at the beginning of this chapter. (The boy admitted later from his hospital bed that he'd bumped an underwater obstruction and knocked his face plate loose.) So let's learn right now how easy it is to remove the water from a flooded mask without surfacing.

Chapter Two explained the use of the snorkel and emphasized the need for properly fitted foot fins. Put on your fins. Notice how awkward they feel as you walk with high, deliberate steps toward the water. Never try to run while wearing the flippers.

Walk backwards when you enter the shallow water. The supple fins offer less resistance and have less chance of tripping you that way. Take a few strokes and observe how much easier it is to swim with the fins. They will increase your normal swimming speed about one-third. You will discover that underwater the fins provide so much extra power you need not use your arms. You can swim with your hands held back against your sides, or stretched straight ahead to ward off obstructions in murky water. Trying to stroke with the arms while submerged only increases fatigue and air consumption without appreciably increasing your speed.

Toss your mask into fairly deep water and let it sink to the bottom. Take a good breath, dive down, and put the flooded face plate back on. Look surfaceward and, holding the top of the mask firmly against your forehead with both hands, exhale steadily through the nose. The air entering the face plate will occupy the upper portion, forcing the water out at the bottom. You can actually observe the water level dropping before your blurred eyes as you continue to exhale until clear vision is restored. It's that simple.

As you return to the surface, remember the SCUBA diver's rule to pause briefly about six feet down to look and listen in all directions for danger above. A sharp blow on the head from a pier or floating object overhead can be painful. Worse, a boat may be approaching. A spinning propeller can make hamburger of a skin diver.

Now let's try it again, but this time, instead of looking surfaceward to clear the mask, remain submerged as you swim with face toward the bottom. Roll your body a half turn, to face right or left. Press one hand against whichever side is at the top of the

Instructor has student remove her face plate to show how to clear flooded mask under water properly.

Student, looking at instructor as he prevents her from rising, prepares to put flooded mask in position.

Student uses one hand to hold mask seal tight against forehead to force water from bottom of flooded mask.

Asked by instructor's hand signal if she can see clearly one more, she replies with signal, "Yes, okay."

As you return to the surface, remember the SCUBA diver's rule to pause briefly about six feet down to look and listen in all directions for danger from above.

mask. Hold it thus, firmly against your face, as you exhale steadily to clear the face plate as before.

Next, return to the bottom with both mask and snorkel in position. Lift one edge of the rubber face plate border to flood the mask. Then use only a *part* of your breath to clear the mask, the remaining air to clear the snorkel as you surface without lifting your head from the water.

You will probably need to practice this last procedure more than the others. If necessary, you can increase your breath capacity by taking several deep breaths in succession, exhaling each one all the way, immediately before submerging, holding the last one for use while below, of course. Such "hyperventilation" provides your lungs with more than the normal amount of oxygen, and you can stay down longer. It is standard procedure among snorkel divers.

You've been practicing swimming with the customary skin diver's "flutter kick," a simple up-and-down leg movement from the hips instead of the knees. If you wish, you can switch now and then to the scissors kick for a change of pace. A change of pace is in order now. You should never tire yourself when skin diving; always hold some strength in reserve—you may need it. So let's dry off and learn some more about pressure effects.

An empty metal can, sealed airtight, weighted and lowered into deep water, will reach a critical depth where the weight of the water, pressing in upon the can from all sides, would exceed the resisting pressure of the air trapped inside. The can would be crushed, just as a man's chest would be crushed unless he managed to build up an increasing air pressure inside his lungs to prevent this as he descended to such dangerous depths.

Fortunately, as we have learned, your sensitive SCUBA regulator constantly balances or equalizes your mouthpiece, and lung, air pressure with the surrounding water pressure upon the regulator and your body. The happy result is that we will not be crushed like the tin can.

This is the reason the SCUBA user can descend to depths that would prove disastrous for an ordinary skin diver. However, let me warn you against trying to overdo it when you graduate to SCUBA gear. I must strongly urge that you never exceed 130 feet. It would be better if you set for yourself a limit of one hundred, and there is seldom need for an amateur diver to go to that depth. Many instructors ask students to remain at thirty feet or less until they've been diving for a full year. Even at depths less than one hundred feet, some divers are apt to show beginning signs of drunkenness from nitrogen narcosis, the "rapture of the deep," which can cause the diver to lose all sense of direction, happily descending even deeper to certain death instead of returning surfaceward. At the first indication of this, you should ascend immediately to a level where such light-headedness disappears.

Another danger of deep diving is decompression illness, better known as "the bends." Nitrogen bubbles form in the blood stream as a result of ascending too rapidly without proper decompression stops on the way up after prolonged or repeated dives. Fortunately, decompression illness need not claim you if you will use the U.S. Navy Decompression Table (see pp. 48-49) to plan each deep dive carefully beforehand. You can determine from the table how fast you should return to the surface for a given descent time plus the time spent on the bottom.

Whatever may prove your favorite type of diving, it is important that you understand the need of and use of the decompression table. Whether you prefer to explore for gold or other valuable salvage, indulge in underwater rockhounding, or even hire out, you must never forget that should you exceed certain critical times and depths during your diving, it is imperative you deliberately wait at certain predetermined levels during your return to the surface. This is stage decompression, and failure to decompress invites the "bends."

So long as you do not ascend faster than your bubbles, about twenty-five feet per minute, you can operate at depths up to thirty feet with no concern for decompression. From thirty to forty feet, you can remain down a total of 120 minutes without making provision for decompression. And remember that by remaining "down" means bottom time *plus* the time spent in descending. This no-decompression time will reduce to but fifteen minutes for depths of 120 to 130 feet.

If you plan to exceed the critical "down" time, it is a simple matter to refer to the table as you plan your dive *beforehand,* to learn at what depth you must pause, and for how long, on the way up. For instance, referring to the table, if you dove to seventy feet and spent a total of ninety minutes on the bottom, including your descent time, the table calls for a wait on your way up for four minutes at a depth of twenty feet and again for sixteen minutes at the 10-foot depth. This makes a total decompression period of about twenty-four minutes, allowing four minutes for you to swim up from the bottom. Should you spend ninety minutes down on a 130-foot dive, your total decompression time will increase almost six times, with prolonged stops at the 40-, 30-, 20- and 10-foot levels. Don't take chances by cutting corners.

Dives should be carefully planned, using U.S. Navy Decompression Tables where necessary to determine maximum time that can safely be spent on the bottom.

These tables have been worked out by U.S. Navy experts and are used by divers around the world.

It is possible that an emergency can arise that will keep you from meeting the table's requirements. You have no alternative then but to allow yourself to be rushed to the nearest land or shipboard recompression station where you must "sweat it out" in a sealed steel chamber uncomfortably hot from the compressed air which roars in your ears and "brings you back" from the depths. That is, the air pressure on your body is adjusted to simulate what it should have been in equivalent water pressure had you observed the proper delay periods for a normal decompression ascent from the depths. Under severe conditions, this may take a full day or more.

Ricou Browning, the strong-swimming underwater actor who first gained recognition in his Hollywood movie roles as the "Creature of the Black Lagoon" and later served as underwater supervisor for "Sea Hunt" and other TV productions, recently related a recompression chamber experience to the author.

"Lamar Boren, the famed cameraman who filmed the underwater sequences for 'The Old Man and the Sea' and many other movies, needed some footage of sharks in their natural surroundings. To provide this, we arranged for him to work near a emergency steel shark cage, with spare compressed air tanks at his elbow.

"For two weeks we daily lowered the cage into tropic water while we hopefully baited the bottom with thousands of pounds of fresh fish, and the actors swam about before the camera, waiting for the sharks to appear.

"Finally the brutes suddenly showed up in droves late one afternoon. They began to tear up the bait on the bottom like dogs tearing up rags. I watched one especially vicious 15-foot hammerhead repeatedly chase off the others, although he chose to eat little himself. He seemed to have his eye on me and two companions.

"At last Boren signaled that he'd gotten the footage we needed. We'd have no recompression problem because we could enter the cage and those on the boat above could raise the cage slowly. But it was fast getting dark. We headed for the surface and safety. But I had made too many dives too deep that day, and had not followed the repetitive diving charts correctly. I had become so engrossed in our work I had made that error of stupidity.

"That evening my shoulders began to ache. The pain spread and grew worse. A plane was summoned by radio, and I was rushed to the Navy base at Key West. There I was quickly placed in a recompression chamber. Fortunately, I suffered no bad results."

In diving deep you should always use decompression tables, and it should be every SCUBA devotee's responsibility to learn beforehand the location of the nearest recompression chamber in case an emergency should arise. But nothing is so important that you can't follow the decompression tables—experience is a great teacher.

Bill Ray, a veteran SCUBA diver of many years despite his youth, relates this harrowing experience as proof of the need for planning each deep dive, and never making one without a buddy:

"Because the glass-clear water at Florida's Silver Springs permits convenient study and photography of new aquatic products, it has long served as the initial testing site for such items. Years ago, shortly after the early self-contained diving lungs began to show up at the Springs for testing (the first one was a Spato, made in Canada), three of us decided to make use of these outfits to explore a seemingly bottomless waterhole on a horse ranch at nearby Ocala, Florida.

"I arrived at the appointed time, but the two other divers were not there. I waited. Word of what we intended to do had gotten around and a crowd had collected to watch. After a while, I could sense that the onlookers were becoming impatient, perhaps wondering if I'd lost my nerve as my absent companions seemed to have done.

"I did a foolish thing. Rather than disappoint the crowd I decided to dive alone.

"The water proved to be very murky, and the daylight was quickly blotted out as I lowered myself into the rocky fault and groped my way downward along the rough face of a sheer limestone wall. I kept going lower and lower. But nothing seemed to change. There just remained that grim rocky wall before me.

"I was in total darkness. I couldn't distinguish my hands held close to my face mask. After awhile I seemed to lose track of time, of reality. I wasn't sure whether I was going up or down. I hadn't taken time to rig a safety return line to the surface. That wasn't the only precaution I'd neglected . . .

"I began to grapple with panic.

"I thought of placing my hand over the bubbling regulator behind my head to determine the direction being taken by the escaping air. *That,* surely, would prove conclusively which end was up: the bubbles would be moving surfaceward.

UNITED STATES NAVY DECOMPRESSION TABLES

(for Compressed Air)

1	2	3									4	5
	Time on	Stops (feet and minutes)									Sum of times at various	Approximate total decompression
Depth of dive (feet)	bottom (minutes)	Feet 90	Feet 80	Feet 70	Feet 60	Feet 50	Feet 40	Feet 30	Feet 20	Feet 10	stops (minutes)	time (minutes)
40....	120	....	....	....	....	....	....	....	....	0	0	2
40....	180	....	....	....	....	....	....	....	....	2	2	4
40....	Opt.* 240	....	....	....	....	....	....	....	....	4	4	6
40....	300	....	....	....	....	....	....	....	....	6	6	8
50....	78	....	....	....	....	....	....	....	....	0	0	2
50....	120	....	....	....	....	....	....	....	....	2	2	5
50....	Opt.* 190	....	....	....	....	....	....	....	....	9	9	12
50....	300	....	....	....	....	....	....	....	....	12	12	15
60....	55	....	....	....	....	....	....	....	....	0	0	3
60....	75	....	....	....	....	....	....	....	....	2	2	5
60....	110	....	....	....	....	....	....	....	....	13	13	16
60....	Opt.* 150	....	....	....	....	....	....	....	5	15	20	24
60....	180	....	....	....	....	....	....	....	7	16	23	27
60....	210	....	....	....	....	....	....	....	8	18	26	30
70....	43	....	....	....	....	....	....	....	....	0	0	3
70....	60	....	....	....	....	....	....	....	....	4	4	8
70....	90	....	....	....	....	....	....	....	4	16	20	24
70....	Opt.* 120	....	....	....	....	....	....	....	13	16	29	33
70....	150	....	....	....	....	....	....	....	18	21	39	43
70....	180	....	....	....	....	....	....	....	21	32	53	57
80....	35	....	....	....	....	....	....	....	....	0	0	3
80....	50	....	....	....	....	....	....	....	....	6	6	10
80....	70	....	....	....	....	....	....	....	6	16	22	27
80....	100	....	....	....	....	....	....	....	20	16	36	41
80....	Opt.* 115	....	....	....	....	....	....	....	22	26	48	53
80....	150	....	....	....	....	....	....	....	28	29	57	62
90....	30	....	....	....	....	....	....	....	....	0	0	4
90....	45	....	....	....	....	....	....	....	....	6	6	10
90....	60	....	....	....	....	....	....	....	9	16	25	30
90....	75	....	....	....	....	....	....	....	18	14	32	37
90....	Opt.* 95	....	....	....	....	....	....	2	27	21	50	56
90....	130	....	....	....	....	....	....	9	27	29	65	71
100....	25	....	....	....	....	....	....	....	....	0	0	4
100....	40	....	....	....	....	....	....	....	....	12	12	17
100....	60	....	....	....	....	....	....	....	18	16	34	39
100....	75	....	....	....	....	....	....	....	27	21	48	53
100....	Opt.* 85	....	....	....	....	....	....	6	28	21	55	61
100....	90	....	....	....	....	....	....	8	27	24	59	65
100....	120	....	....	....	....	....	....	17	28	48	93	99
110....	20	....	....	....	....	....	....	....	....	0	0	5
110....	35	....	....	....	....	....	....	....	....	12	12	17
110....	55	....	....	....	....	....	....	....	22	21	43	49
110....	Opt.* 75	....	....	....	....	....	....	14	27	37	78	84
110....	105	....	....	....	....	....	2	22	29	50	103	110
120....	18	....	....	....	....	....	....	....	....	0	0	5
120....	30	....	....	....	....	....	....	....	....	11	11	17
120....	45	....	....	....	....	....	....	....	18	21	39	45

1	2	3									4	5
Depth of dive (feet)	Time on bottom (minutes)	Stops (feet and minutes)									Sum of times at various stops (minutes)	Approximate total decompression time (minutes)
		Feet 90	Feet 80	Feet 70	Feet 60	Feet 50	Feet 40	Feet 30	Feet 20	Feet 10		
120....	Opt.* 65							13	28	32	73	80
120....	100						5	22	27	69	123	130
130....	15									0	0	5
130....	35								11	15	26	32
130....	52							6	28	28	62	69
130....	Opt.* 60							13	28	28	69	76
130....	90						9	22	28	69	128	136
140....	15									4	4	10
140....	30								8	21	29	36
140....	45							5	27	27	59	67
140....	Opt.* 55							15	28	32	75	82
140....	85						14	22	32	69	137	145
150....	15									7	7	14
150....	30								13	21	34	41
150....	38								28	30	58	65
150....	Opt.* 50							16	28	32	76	84
150....	80						18	23	32	69	141	150
160....	15									9	9	16
160....	34								27	28	55	63
160....	Opt.* 45							17	28	43	88	96
160....	75					3	19	23	34	68	147	156
170....	15									11	11	18
170....	30								24	27	51	59
170....	Opt.* 40							19	28	46	93	102
170....	75					9	19	23	38	68	157	167
185....	15									25	25	33
185....	26								24	37	61	70
185....	Opt.* 35							19	28	46	93	102
185....	65				18	18	23	37	65	51	212	223
200....	15									32	32	41
200....	23								23	37	60	69
200....	Opt.* 35							22	28	46	96	106
200....	60			5	18	18	23	37	65	51	217	229
210....	15									35	35	44
210....	Opt.* 30						5	16	28	40	89	100
210....	55			6	18	18	23	37	65	51	218	231
225....	15								6	35	41	51
225....	Opt.* 27						22	26	35	48	131	143
225....	60			13	18	18	23	47	65	83	267	280
250....	15								17	37	54	66
250....	Opt.* 25					2	23	26	35	51	137	150
250....	50		12	14	17	19	29	49	65	83	288	303
300....	12								20	37	57	70
300....	Opt.* 20					9	23	26	35	51	144	159
300....	45	6	14	15	17	18	31	49	65	83	298	315

* These are the optimum exposure times for each depth which represent the best balance between length of work period and amount of useful work for the average diver. Exposure beyond these times is permitted only under special conditions.

49

"Fortunately, however, I decided not to do this . . .

"What seemed hours later I groped my way back to the surface of the small hole, shivering and nearly exhausted. By this time one of the other two divers had arrived.

" 'What happened down there?' he asked, looking at me strangely. 'I was watching your bubbles. Then they disappeared for quite a long while.'

"This shocked me. I knew now what had happened: I'd wandered beneath a subterranean ledge and into a connecting cavern. North-central Florida is honeycombed with such flooded passageways. Had I used my escaping air bubbles to determine which direction was up, I very likely would have climbed higher into that inky black tomb—never to find my way back."

We've shown how the sealed tin can would be crushed in the depths; now here is another noteworthy example of pressure effects that directly concern a diver. Let's assume we inflate a child's rubber balloon in deep water and release it there. The balloon would expand and burst before it reached the surface. Reason: the pressure (weight) of the water upon the balloon will decrease as it ascends until the point is reached where the air pressure inside becomes so great by comparison it explodes. Remember, it required considerable air pressure in the first place to blow up the balloon against the pressure of the surrounding water in the depths. In similar manner, a man's lungs would be damaged from over-expansion or "air embolism" if he held his breath while ascending after diving with SCUBA. As a skin diver using properly operating compressed air apparatus you will experience no difficulty from air embolism, however, if you will remember to ascend in a leisurely manner, no faster than your smallest air bubbles and continue to breathe normally while doing this.

Should your equipment fail for some reason, forcing you to ditch it and make an emergency or "free" ascent relying only upon what air may be left in your lungs at the time, you *must* exhale all the way up to avoid air embolism. Remember to increase the rate of your exhalation as you near the surface, since the greatest change in surrounding water pressure takes place there. This is easier than it sounds—you can exhale effortlessly for a long time as the air in your lungs expands.

Bear in mind that it is not necessary to make deep dives before you need concern yourself with the danger of air embolism. It can take place in ten feet of water. And often it gives no warning symptoms.

These two potentially dangerous diver's pressure effects which result from descending and ascending without equalizing internal and external body pressures have their basis in Boyle's law, which states that if the pressure of a gas is cut in half, the volume is doubled, and vice versa.

Now that you've become familiar with basic snorkeling equipment, let's get a good night of rest and return to our shallow lake in the morning, refreshed and ready to don full SCUBA gear.

"You must fill tanks like these only with pure, filtered, compressed air—not oxygen or any other gas," explains the attendant as we carry twin SCUBA outfits into the local air depot next morning. "You purchase such air at regular supply stations such as this, or perhaps a skin diving equipment store—but never at the corner filling station."

He explains that the corner gas station not only hasn't sufficient pressure to fill a compressed air tank, but also that such air isn't pure enough for you to breathe. Lubricating oil can dangerously contaminate such air with carbon monoxide. So, for that matter, can an approved skin diver's compressor unit should it be carelessly placed so that its air intake is downwind from the engine exhaust. This is the same carbon monoxide poisoning that can sneak up and overpower you in a closed garage with a motor running. But pressure makes the effects much worse.

Our single 70-cubic-foot tanks are each equipped with a constant reserve valve. The reserve is a great safety factor. Should you forget the time and use up all your air, you can reach back with one hand to operate an easily reached pull-rod. This will release enough reserve air to get you safely back to the surface; about two to six minutes worth, depending upon depth and the work performed.

Each tank is filled to 2,250 p.s.i. You notice that before he feeds your tank from a series of large, connected storage tanks in his shop, the attendant first immerses it in water to keep it cool. The SCUBA tank will develop considerable heat during the filling process.

Your tank full, its valve is closed securely. The feed line and its gauge are disconnected and the tank's reserve supply valve is placed in the up position, ready for use. The regulator is next attached and all hoses, valves and surfaces of the SCUBA given a close inspection for damage and leaks.

"Now reopen the tank valve and insert the mouthpiece between your teeth to see if you can inhale and exhale," the attendant invites. You do this and discover that the operation is not difficult although it calls for a definite "demand" on your part for each breath. You turn off the air supply and we are ready to get underway.

We carry the filled tanks carefully to our waiting station wagon—*not* by the valve housings—and place the bottles so the tops of the tanks face toward the rear. That way if we must stop quickly there will be less chance of damaging the valves should the tanks slide forward. Nor should a filled tank ever be stood

The regulator is attached and all hoses, valves and surfaces of the SCUBA given close inspection.

Carry the tanks carefully, not by the valve housing.

upright without support, so there is danger of its falling over and damaging its valve. There is on record at least one case where compressed air escaping from a broken-off SCUBA tank valve sent the heavy steel tank hurtling through the air like a projectile for three city blocks, and then through the side of a house!

Outdoors, particularly while you may be waiting to use it, leave your SCUBA in the shade whenever possible since the sun's heat will further increase the pressure. Also, sun deteriorates the rubber mouthpieces and hoses.

Since you are a beginner, I will help you slip on your SCUBA harness. Whether it consists of backpack or straps only, all webbing buckles and knots must—like your weight belt—be of the quick-release type. Remember that the weight belt goes on *last* so it can be released first, with one hand, if you must surface quickly in an emergency.

With fins and mask on, snorkel tube secured to mask headstrap (you will want to use the snorkel later to conserve compressed air

Place the bottles so the tops of the tanks face toward the rear of the trunk of your car.

while swimming at the surface), reach behind and turn on the tank valve for a final check that your mouthpiece is delivering air properly.

Leave the valve open and walk into the water backward to chest depth. With mouthpiece in position, settle yourself on the bottom while you familiarize yourself with inhaling and exhaling underwater. If your belt weight is right for neutral buoyancy, you will feel yourself move upward slightly from the bottom each time you inhale, then settle back again as you exhale. After a few minutes of this, flood your face plate. Note how much easier it is to clear the mask, now that you have an unlimited supply of air available.

It is even more important that you know how to clear your mouthpiece should it flood for some reason and prevent you from drawing air through it without choking on water at the same time. So remove it from your mouth and deliberately let it become filled.

Should you drop the mouthpiece, face surfaceward so it will float directly overhead, within easy reach as it bubbles escaping air. Should it become trapped under your back while in a horizontal position, roll over to free it.

It is a characteristic of the sensitive SCUBA regulator that the greater the depth difference existing between it and its mouth-piece, the stronger will be the flow of air escaping from the mouthpiece. This is exactly what you want, i.e., to insure that water will occupy a minimum space in the mouthpiece, so hold the mouthpiece as far over your head as possible. Then, with its opening facing downward, bring the mouthpiece down quickly into position and clamp your teeth over it. Roll onto your back so gravity will pull any remaining water down through the hose toward the regulator until you can draw your first breath.

Should you discover some troublesome water still left in the mouthpiece, use your remaining body air to exhale, blowing this water sharply out through the exhaust hose's non-return valve, meanwhile rolling your body to the left to aid this action, since the exhaust tube is the left one if you are using a double hose regulator. If you have no air left in your lungs to do this, it is best to swallow the small amount of water remaining before at-tempting to draw your first breath from the mouthpiece. Be careful not to choke—a cough can be a big project.

Older model SCUBAs did not employ non-return valves in their air hoses and were more difficult to clear when the mouth-piece flooded. You had to roll from right to left, i.e., counterclock-wise, letting gravity pull the blocking water down into the exhaust tube as you exhaled; sometimes continuing the roll full onto your back while stretching the exhaust hose and exhaling. This method should be practiced should you ever be obliged to use a SCUBA not equipped with non-return valves.

So far you've learned to use snorkel and SCUBA and to clear flooded face plate and mouthpiece. Now I want you to "dress out" underwater. That is, leave your full equipment on the bottom, as you might in an emergency ditching, then dive down and put it on again.

Here we go: dive to the bottom and sit there as before. Remove weight belt, placing it across your legs to help hold you down. Release the instant-release webbing knots of your harness. Reach back and lift the loosened tank over your head, keeping the mouthpiece in position for continued breathing.

Place the tank between your knees until you can drape the weight belt over it. If your fins are the floating type, tuck them

Example of "dressing out" underwater.

under the tank so the weight belt will hold them against the bottom, too.

Assume a prone position, facing the tank and regulator, and take a final breath. Turn off tank valve. Place mouthpiece between valve and regulator, to secure it there. Swim *slowly* to surface, remembering to exhale all the way up, increasing the rate as you near the surface.

When you've rested at the top, make a surface dive and return to the ditched equipment. Once more assume a prone position with lungs at approximately the same level as the mouthpiece wedged between regulator and valve.

Turn on the tank valve. Hold the mouthpiece well above the regulator to insure a strong flow of escaping air. Point it downward, bringing it quickly down into your mouth. Hold the exhaust hose low to gravity-aid the clearance of any blocking water left in the mouthpiece as you exhale sharply to clear it.

As you resume normal breathing, straddle the tank, gripping it with one knee on each side. Remove the weight belt from the tank and drape it across your legs. Hold the tank near its top and swing it over your head into position. Fasten its harness in the approved quick-release fashion. Replace fins and weight belt and you are ready to go on your way beneath the surface.

One more lesson—this time how to render assistance to other divers—and we are ready to swim off together to enjoy some underwater exploring.

The diving fraternity will expect you to help a fellow diver in distress wherever and whenever you may encounter him in trouble. You should be able to size up the situation quickly, yet calmly. He may only be exhausted and grateful for an assist to shore. Or he may be crazed from lack of air, ready to act as violently as any other person in danger of drowning. In this case, you must approach him cautiously offering him your float as you use logic to calm him down and bring him ashore. Remember that if you carelessly allow yourself to become a victim to the same circumstances, neither of you will benefit.

A diver who is conscious but too weak to make it safely to shore alone can be towed on his back, just as you towed me during our qualification test. Remove his face plate and weight belt. Inflate his body float to aid you and your own, too, if neces-

To demonstrate "buddy breathing" technique to student, instructor has her release her mouthpiece while she draws air from his.

sary. Should he or you have a surface float handy pull him part way out of the water onto this, with mouth and nose out of water, as you use it to tow him ashore.

Should the victim *not* be breathing when you chance upon him, do not waste precious time towing him ashore. You *must* get air into his lungs immediately. If he is not violent, move in close, wrap your arms about his chest, alternately squeezing and releasing to cause forced breathing. If this doesn't cause him to resume breathing, take a deep breath, place your mouth to his in a tight seal, and literally "blow him up" as you tread water and hold him afloat. Then squeeze this air from him with your arms and repeat. If he doesn't blow up easily, check his throat for a blocking obstruction.

Get him ashore as quickly as possible and continue the artificial respiration there under more favorable conditions. Don't give up until a qualified person pronounces the victim dead. Sometimes artificial respiration must be administered for several hours.

The victim's air may fail in the depths. If he is still conscious when you reach him, let him share your mouthpiece, the two of you alternately breathing from it (clearing it each time as already described) as you return slowly to the surface together. To do this, face each other, each using one hand to hold the other person close during the ascent. Take a deep breath from your working SCUBA and hand him the mouthpiece with your free hand, meanwhile holding your head to the left so your exhaust hose will be low.

If the victim is unconscious when you reach him in the depths, there is little you can do except get him to the surface quickly as possible and begin mouth-to-mouth artificial respiration as already described. Should there be compressed air locked inside him, he may be subject to air embolism, even the bends, as a result of such abnormal ascent.

We've discussed how the diver's flag is an important safety item, its use recognized internationally today. It is no trick to make your own flag. In fact, it's almost as easy to make several while you're at it to insure a good supply on hand.

Select pieces of strong red cloth that can withstand repeated wetting and exposure to sun without undue fading and rotting. The approved flag should measure either twelve, twenty-one or thirty-three inches square, and should boast a white diagonal stripe that is one-fifth the width of the flag in width. The stripe (which usually consists of a strip of white cloth sewn onto the red background) should extend from the top of the hoist to the bottom of the fly.

The Underwater Society of America recommends that the 12-inch flag be flown from a diver's float of the one- or two-man size;

The diver's flag should be flown whenever you are in the water.

the 21-inch flag from diving boats up to forty feet in length; the large flag for boats to eighty feet.

The float flag may be supported by a 3-foot high mast of wood, metal, or cane fastened to a suitable small float at the base of the standard which is in turn anchored to the bottom with a stout cord and suitable weight whenever the diver is below. To make such a float, you can use solid or hollow wood, or flat pieces of cork glued together. If you wish, the float may be shaped into a

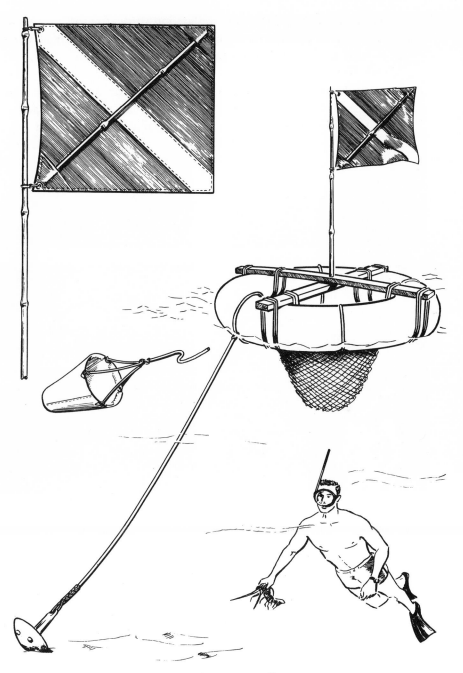

It is no trick to make your own flag.

streamlined capsule. Don't use a glass jug since it is easily broken.

The mast is passed through the center of the float or secured to it with cord or other means.

The diver's flag should be flown whenever you are in the water. It tells all boatmen that you are requesting one hundred feet of clearance, hence you should surface only at the flag location. Even then, do so cautiously; a boat may not have seen your flag.

4. Exploring and Collecting Underwater

Before we leave on that exploring trip I promised in the last chapter, let's make final equipment checks. Is there an ample supply of clean compressed air in your tank, as read by a removable pressure gauge? Every SCUBA diver should have access to one. Do the regulators work properly when tank valves are turned on? Can all diving-equipment surfaces pass close inspection for cuts and other visible damage, including a rubber suit if it is to be used? Have you packed your mask, snorkel, fins, weight belt, knife, body and surface floats, and diver's flag? Take along also a wrist-type depth gauge and, if you own one, a waterproof watch and compass.

A first-aid kit will prove handy for minor cuts and bruises from rocks and shells, perhaps stings and other small wounds by jellyfish, sea urchins, sting rays, and others. A check list is a big help in organizing your gear.

"Where shall we find water for diving?" you may ask, since that is the inevitable beginner's question.

The answer is easy. Where *can't* we go? Water makes up two-thirds of the earth's surface. Since we're trained to be human fish, we should be right at home wherever there is water. If you are in the mood for a lark, we can drive out to the local country club and, after requesting permission to dive, salvage armfuls of golf balls from the water hazards. The best-preserved of these we can sell back to the pro or the caddy store.

Perhaps you'd prefer to visit the yacht club or the fishing docks. Some skipper there is bound to be grateful for a free inspection for possible hull damage. Or perhaps he'd like us to remove a length of rope or wire he knows has become wrapped about a propeller shaft.

Every SCUBA diver should have a pressure gauge.

You are free to dive in any bay, river, lake or other calm water where you're not likely to encounter dangerous currents and fish, underwater obstructions that might entangle and cut you, or hazardous boat traffic. Even a man-made canal or rock quarry will do, although such landlocked sites usually offer muddy and monotonous bottoms. Such stagnant, silted water is also easily stirred up by a diver's flippers—and this can result in ear infections.

Let's assume we live near the ocean and try it. The sea is usually the cleanest water, and there are beaches for easy access.

We have aptly described ourselves as human fish. But don't forget that when you're dressed in full SCUBA gear you are also much like a fish—out of water. It is easy to fall and hurt both yourself and your equipment. The danger therefore from undertow, entangling kelp and other growths, floating debris and other obstacles should be obvious. If the surf is heavy, wait for a calmer time or dive inland or in sheltered waters. You could be thrown against something—even your buddy—and be hurt.

If you must climb among rocks or across slippery surfaces to reach or leave the water, it is best to leave your equipment safely behind first while you make a scouting trip.

Any skipper would be grateful for free inspection of his boat.

You are free to dive in any bay, river, lake or other calm water.

Today, however, we will assume that the ocean is calm. Warm sand crunches musically beneath your webbed feet as we turn on our air supplies and walk backwards into the waves. Were we entering the water from a boat or dock we'd have the choice of "rolling off" backward or jumping in feet first. In either case, the distance to the water surface shouldn't be more than about six feet, and your hands should be used to hold mask and tank firmly in position against the shock.

And now you are under at last, for your first dive in open water. How big and strange this new world looks and feels and sounds as you hang in "hydrospace" above it! You catch yourself working your arms and feet nervously fast for a few seconds lest you fall down into the mysterious depths. But have no fear. With your weight belt adjusted for neutral buoyancy, you couldn't fall if you tried.

Our diver's flag floats on the surface, warning any approaching boats that we are diving in this area. So let's go. Down, down, down we slowly kick our way into this new fantasy world of shimmering green light . . . pumping easily from the hips and clearing our ears as necessary.

Your eyes widen as you try to take it all in at once—and fail. As we glide along in the strange, soft light, your ever shifting glance picks out shadowy rocks below, fish and undersea growths. Sounds are amplified. There is the rhythmic rush of compressed air in your ears. You hear the snaps, pops and cracklings of this big bowl of underwater cereal. A fish, looming larger than life in the magnifying water, swims lazily past you and you *know* you heard this fellow breathing! Sound travels several times better and faster through water than it does through the air of our surface world.

A whole school of tiny, brightly colored fish now swirls unexpectedly about us, startling you briefly before they flash away again. I watch your reaction across a dozen yards of intervening water and join thumb and first finger of one hand in a circle to inquire if you are okay. You reply "yes" using the same hand signal for, as part of your "homework," you have learned the basic signals which SCUBA divers use communicating underwater.

Underwater communication remains a vexing problem. In ad-

The diver may roll off backward from boat or pier.

dition to these hand signals, there are standardized sound and rope signals to be used when necessary. One tap with knife on tank, for example, or a single pull on a rope, means "I am okay." Three double taps or pulls in succession warns "I need help." Four serve as a request to be pulled up at once—or, when sent down from the surface, this becomes an order to come up.

In this bubbling never-never land, we have realized man's oldest dream and escaped gravity. You realize this is the closest you will ever come to flying without wings.

A large rock, covered with a miniature forest of green vegetation, passes immediately below. You can see several fish hovering motionless about its down-current side. These fellows know that such obstructions afford a stopping and growing place for small plants and minute marine animals which little fish feed upon. Larger fish, in turn, feed upon such small fry.

I signal you that we will go down and take a closer look. We make it a point to approach from the down-current side ourselves—not to observe the fish, but so the current won't sweep us against the rough rock, or into a crevice, should it prove that strong. It isn't, and as we approach, you will notice that the motionless fish show no fear of us. If you had a speargun along, you could bring some of them home for dinner. (We'll go fishing a couple of chapters later.) You point excitedly at a lobster's twin feelers protruding from a fissure. But the "bug," as divers call him, ducks safely from sight before your reaching hands can close upon him. We move on. Overhead the bright surface of the sea seems far away. But a glance at your wrist gauge assures you it's only twenty-five feet.

On a sandy patch of bottom, we come upon a short length of frayed rope, one end disappearing into the sand. It floats lazily upward, undulating gently in the current like some ghostly finger from the past. We try to pull up the rope, taking turns, but can't. You'll never know what, if anything, was fastened to the other end.

The bottom contour changes as we slip across a looming reef with patches of scarlet coral and into a valley. The floor is cov-

The diver has the choice of jumping in feet first when entering the water.

ered with starfish and shells and the whitest of sand. You can hear the shells chinking together clearly with each surge of the current. We begin to gather cones and angel wings and what not, wishing we hadn't forgotten to bring along a couple of sacks. Once, as you move close to inspect a beautiful growth of elkhorn coral, I pull you back. It is poisonous and can produce a painful infection. You'll need some more homework on dangerous marine growths and animals.

School after school of the little rainbow-hued fish now descend upon us again. They seem to come from all directions and remind me of two Florida divers who have worked up a lucrative business supplying such specimens on order to aquariums and pet shops around the nation. They comb reefs where the tiny tropic fish swarm, catching them with hand nets.

Treasure of one sort or another is the big appeal for most skin divers. Tucked away in the back of the SCUBA man's mind is always the secret hope that some day he will come upon something of big value waiting there in the green void below. What can you do to help make this dream a reality?

First, pay little attention to the inevitable accounts of pirate maps, secret codes and such. You can always readily find someone who "knows" where treasure lies buried, or knows someone else who supposedly has the secret. If such people knew the location of unclaimed wealth, it's hardly likely they'd be letting you in on it.

On the other hand, old shipping manifests and similar historic documents will confirm that staggering amounts of the world's lost riches have never been reclaimed. Most of it is in gold and silver that went to the bottom in shipwrecks. The serious treasure hunter constantly seeks out leads from such reliable information, checking these against present-day circumstances. He does this quietly, sometimes even furtively, like an inventor working upon a secret project. When he does decide to dive at a possible site, he usually tries to act like an innocent fisherman or vacationist, refusing to say where he *and his partner* are hunting or if he has found anything.

"You'd do the same," a treasure hunter once told the author. "If not, you'd find yourself swamped with insurance claims, law-

Hand signals for asking, "are you okay?" You reply, "Yes," with the proper signal.

suits from heirs—even the danger of being hijacked, and I don't mean just by the Government for income taxes!"

In the author's home state of Florida, historic records reveal that a Spanish treasure fleet, heavy-laden with gold plundered from Mexico, foundered in a storm almost within sight of what is now Miami. As the high-pooped galleons rent their bottoms against knife-sharp coral reefs and slid beneath the churning waves, they joined more than sixty other doomed vessels already there, some of them pirate ships. Today it is reliably estimated that at least sixty-four million dollars lies hidden beneath the blue waters and shifting sands off the famed vacation city.

Not all this early wealth was lost during storms. Some fifty miles north along the Atlantic coast from Miami, where I live in the palm-grown inlet settlement of Boca Raton, the cruel buccaneer Blackbeard supposedly buried his vast fortune behind the dunes. There is no record of this rich horde ever being found, and now it probably lies sunken in the warm bottom sand a few hundred yards offshore, since the coastline has since eroded steadily in this area.

Other pirates like Gasparilla, Morgan, and Billy Bowlegs are described as having hidden untold wealth in silver, gold and jewels around the islands east of Pensacola. To this day, occasional doubloons are found by tourists walking the beaches after a storm. In 1840 a British gunboat sank a Billy Bowlegs privateer in Apalachee Bay with five million dollars in bar silver aboard. And a hundred miles farther south along this sun-washed Gulf coast, near the Suwannee River, a pirate ship shelled another craft until it sank, taking with it five million dollars in gold and silver that was being sent to Spain in partial payment for the purchase of Florida by the United States.

These and many other authentic losses—like some recoveries— are a matter of available record and should not be confused with the often costly "true" (until you try to prove them!) stories of lost treasure that abound along any waterfront.

For example, about 1935 a fisherman known only as Charlie reportedly dozed off while sailing his small boat near Pigeon Key in the Florida Keys. His unguided craft eventually ran onto a reef, awakening him. Getting out to push the craft off, Charlie found himself standing upon several barnacle-encrusted pigs of metal. Thinking that some of this weight might someday prove useful for sailing ballast, he tossed a couple into the boat. Two years later when he hauled out for repairs, he remembered the metal bars. He was about to discard them when someone suggested he have them analyzed. You guessed it, they proved to be pure silver!

Although he searched long and hard, Charlie never did rediscover the treasure site. And he said the reef was littered for three hundred feet with similar bars! Records show that a schooner was lost off Pigeon Key in 1820 with millions in bar silver aboard and never found. This *could* have been part of the vessel's rich cargo. Maybe.

One confirmed Florida treasure recovery story involves a

Treasure of one sort or another is the big appeal for many skin divers.

SCUBA diver who was searching off Key Largo for old Spanish cannon in 1949. Such cannon, like ancient anchors, are regularly recovered by Florida divers. This SCUBA devotee spotted the remains of a wrecked galleon in about sixty feet of water. Among the ship's ballast he discovered three large silver ingots. After the bars were cleaned of layers of coral crust they were found to weight sixty, seventy and seventy-five pounds. The lucky diver sold the 70-pound ingot to the Smithsonian Institution for one thousand dollars. It was identified as having come from a rich silver mine in Panama that was worked by the Spanish with Indian slaves. Like much antique treasure, it was worth more as an antiquity than as silver.

Such Spanish treasure ships, homeward bound from the plunder of the Caribbean countries, were obliged to pass through the Florida Straits and sail along miles of dangerous coral reefs before swinging eastward toward home. Many were wrecked on the reefs by sudden tropical storms or were set upon by waiting pirates.

That's why Florida's clear waters attract so many treasure hunters.

Of course, gold is where you find it. You need not limit yourself to romantic tropic waters—or even to the ocean, for that matter. If you live in the West, remember that much of this country's early gold mining took place in your area. The locations of the various placer mines are no secret, and it is safe to assume that a percentage of these mine tailings was carried off into nearby streams, lakes and rivers. A SCUBA diver using one of the portable dredges described earlier could conceivably find his effort well worthwhile should he prospect the right bottoms for such gold.

In fact, even if you didn't recover some of this washed-away gold you will find that many of these same Western rivers flowed through the heart of once-flourishing timber operations. Not all the cut logs that were floated downriver reached their destinations; many thousands jammed up and eventually became waterlogged and sank. A diver can often reclaim such well-preserved hardwood and sell it for a tidy price to cabinet shops, boat yards and other willing purchasers.

Diving for fossils, dry though the subject may sound, can provide thrilling adventures for the most avid explorer. This is the hobby of Jack McEarchern, one of the SCUBA men on the staff of Florida's Silver Springs. McEarchern gives this tip: water seems to preserve fossils almost indefinitely, and many of the fossil remains are found in deep springs. The U.S. Geological Survey publishes inexpensive pamphlets that describe the fossil mammals which once roamed the continent. The pamphlets also list spring locations in those states having such waters.

Back during the era of the movie newsreel companies, Bill Ray and Charlie McNab were encouraged to use two of the early SCUBA outfits to explore the main spring at Silver Springs. Some 550,000,000 gallons of water a day gush forth from this huge subterranean cavern to form the Silver River. No skin diver had ever managed to descend the sixty-five feet to the cave mouth, then force his way in against the outrushing torrent.

Equipped with the SCUBAs, the two men succeeded. The spring cavern runs back into the earth's black bowels for nearly one hundred fifty feet before it becomes too narrow for a man's body. Working without lights, Ray and McNab were startled to come upon huge bones, tusks and teeth. The tusks required their combined strength to carry them ashore after they'd surfaced again. And some of the odd teeth measured as large as 4 by 7 by 11 inches.

Scientists identified the tusks as belonging to a Columbian variety of elephant which inhabited the earth between 20,000 and 40,000 years ago. There were also cave bear and camel bones. (At one time camels were abundant in Florida.) It is believed that these strange bones were placed in the cave ages ago by primitive men, before it was Florida. Jack McEarchern later found three crude flint tools there. The first Indian residents of Florida hunted and killed beasts like the sabertooth tiger and giant wolf until those big mammals became extinct some 10,000 years ago.

McEarchern speaks with glowing enthusiasm of his hobby. But he also warns that it can be *very* dangerous for the inexperienced diver. "Cave diving, like night diving, is strictly for qualified SCUBA users with the right equipment," he cautions. "You and your buddy should always have a safety line to the surface, extra air for emergencies, and a safety man or two standing by in full SCUBA gear if needed."

He points out that you can easily become lost in these underground water areas, lights can fail, safety lines can tangle and cut against sharp bends behind you. "But it is the limited nature of his air supply that is most likely to land the amateur diver in trouble," McEarchern says grimly. "He overlooks the fact his air time will be determined, also, by such factors as depth, by how hard he may be working, and by the decompression period he may have to allow for his return to avoid danger of the bends.

"I remember three boys who went down to explore a spring about seventy miles from here. Each one foolishly brought along but a single 70-cubic-foot bottle—enough for a half hour of normal diving at a 30-foot depth. When they entered the cave, they didn't realize it slanted gradually downward. For each additional ten feet it descended, each boy's air supply was automatically decreased five minutes.

"They were dead even as they started . . ."

As a diver you will find yourself bringing home trophies like odd fish and crustaceans, sponges, shells, and marine growths to

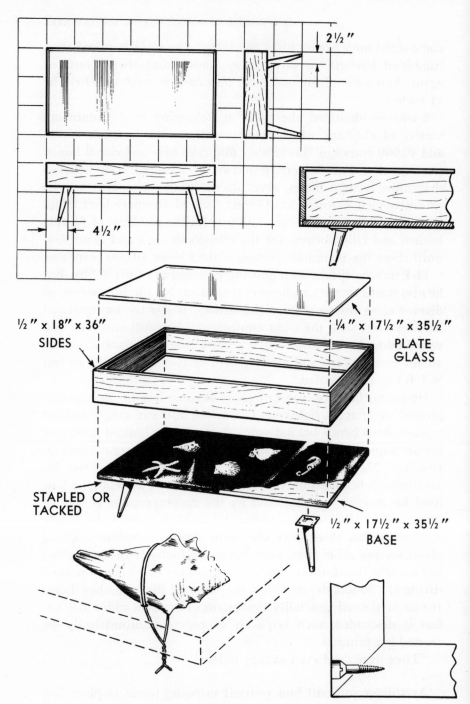

2½"

4½"

½" x 18" x 36"
SIDES

¼" x 17½" x 35½"
PLATE
GLASS

STAPLED OR
TACKED

½" x 17½" x 35½"
BASE

It is easy to make a display board to exhibit your trophies.

show your friends. It is easy to make a display board from which you can exhibit these.

As soon as you return with shells that have living occupants, soak the shells overnight in a solution of formaldehyde and water strong enough to kill. Remove the dead contents later to avoid decay and odor.

Polish and clean your specimens and mount them on a three-by four-foot piece of varnished plywood, or other suitable material, by means of small loops of fine wire. Twist these together behind the board after being passed over the displayed item and through small holes drilled in the mounting board.

Fasten a molding to the panel's outer edges. Coat starfish, small crabs, and so on with varnish. Labels can be lettered or typed upon strips of paper and these glued beneath each mounted object, then varnished over, too.

5. Underwater Photography

We have thrilled to some of the wonders of the underwater world. Now let's photograph these for our friends to enjoy. If you can make an acceptable picture on land, be assured you can do the same underwater—with the same equipment.

To do this, you will need an underwater camera housing. The camera is placed inside a waterproof box and operated by external controls. The project at the end of this chapter will give detailed instructions on how you can build an economical yet dependable underwater box from clear plastic (Plexiglas).

Plexiglas is more fragile than metal. If you *must* scratch it from rough handling, at least spare the transparent section which fits before the camera lens! And it is not suitable for depths much beyond fifty feet. [Metal housings may be safely used to two hundred feet.] It is, however, less expensive and it will provide you with years of good service.

A tip: transparent Plexiglas housings like this can provide sufficient room for mounting a direct-reading light meter of the incident type inside, with the camera. Once set, this type meter will give exposure readings without further adjustment. If your camera leaves no room for the meter, a watertight glass fruit jar secured to your belt with a cord will do nicely for average shallow work.

Don't underestimate the value of an exposure meter. You may be an experienced photographer on dry land, where light is reflected from subject to camera to activate the film. But when you submerge you discover less light reaching the subject. The deeper you go the less light there is. And the light must now travel over *two* paths before it can activate the film: from surface to subject, then from subject to camera.

Photographing two divers digging for buried treasure.

Camera placed inside a Plexiglas box.

The simplest thing is to take a light meter reading near the surface, then a second reading close to the subject, at whatever depth he or it may be. Then, knowing approximately how much light was lost in descending a given distance to the subject, distance as measured by your depth gauge, add to your exposure that *extra* amount which will be lost over the subject-to-camera path.

Any picture, above or below the surface, can be spoiled by such oversights as poor focus, camera movement, use of too slow a shutter speed to stop subject or camera movement, dirty lens, poor composition, faulty equipment and so on. You will find, however, that improper exposure ruins more pictures for the amateur underwater photographer than any of these other mistakes. He will, for example, properly compute exposure for a given depth, then forget to correct against overexposure as he aims upward to catch his buddy returning to the surface where the light often is two stops (lens openings) stronger than that measured fifteen feet below.

For available-light color exposures, you will discover that reds, yellows, oranges and other bright hues are quickly absorbed beneath the surface. The water acts as a very effective color filter. Usually at depths from thirty to one hundred feet, depending upon the natural color of the water in your area, all bright colors have gone, leaving only a flat blue-green. You can sometimes restore this lost color balance to an acceptable degree by using color-correction filters. Or to bring out the really bright submerged colors, despite the depth, you can employ flash or strobe lighting. Caution: due to water refraction the usual flash-

Employing strobe or flash lighting for underwater pictures.

bulb and electronic guide numbers won't prove accurate. You must experiment and establish new guides for your equipment.

A word about filters. Don't make the beginner's mistake of depending upon filters as a substitute for good photography. Bruce Mozert, veteran chief photographer at Florida's Silver Springs, advises you to forget filters, and flash, too, at the outset. In fact, he urges the newcomer to start with an inexpensive box camera and plastic case, total investment about twenty dollars, to see if he will enjoy this new sport before spending more. Mozert, like most expert underwater photographers, uses filters sparingly: perhaps an occasional medium yellow (K2) filter for reducing glare when shooting surfaceward; or an orange (G) to encourage better penetration through water cloudy with tannic acid, as many Florida lakes and streams are.

It is well to keep in mind that the filter does just what its name implies. It filters out—or causes the loss of—some of the natural color in the spectrum of whatever light may be available to you at the moment of exposure. Therefore, to insure optimum exposure of your film (that is, to make certain the necessary amount of light continues to reach the film surface) you must compensate for that loss. This is done by opening the lens aperture wider, to let extra light through to the film (refer to the filter table with your film, showing the necessary increase in exposure), or by decreasing the shutter speed (letting extra light through by increasing the time the lens is held open to make the exposure), or a combination of both of these.

Unfortunately, both these compensating adjustments can jeopardize the effectiveness of the resulting pictures. Opening the lens wider will reduce the depth of field, or zone of sharp focus, to make all fish or other objects except those in the immediate foreground appear hazy and ill-defined. And if you try to reduce shutter speed below the usual minimum of 1/100-second for hand-held exposures, even a slight surge of current against your body can result in picture blur.

You begin to see the limitations. The moment you take a camera underwater, regardless of how shallow the dive may be, you lose light. So why increase the loss of this precious light through careless use of filters?

On the other hand, as we've already indicated, filters do have

These two photos demonstrate how flash lighting can improve the exposure. Note clarity of bottom picture taken with flash, whereas top picture taken under the same conditions, but without flash, has heavy shadows and poor contrast.

a definite place in underwater photography. And, thanks to to-day's much higher speed color and black-and-white films, which require considerably less light to give a good picture, filters are being used in the depths to produce pictures that underwater photographers could only dream of a few years ago.

What, then, determines filter selection? Filters come in several colors; which shall we use? This will depend largely upon the depth at which you must work and the color of your subject. It is characteristic of a photographic filter that it will easily pass its own color, perhaps some others near it in the spectrum, while at the same time offering great opposition to those colors farther removed from it. I've stated that water acts as a filter. As you dive bottomward, you find that yellow, red and other hues present at the surface are quickly absorbed. At one hundred feet—sometimes less—only an over-all blue-green cast remains.

To help restore this upset color balance in the depths we can use a red filter on our camera, for its filtering action is just op-posite that of the water. It permits easy passage of the yellow, red and other water-blocked colors while holding back blue and green. Hence by using it we tend to equalize once more the amplitude of the various color frequencies reaching our film—even though the total amplitude of such twice-attenuated light is now considerably less than it was at the surface, calling for increased lens opening, or slower shutter speed, or both, as al-ready discussed.

Other color filter combinations are possible to meet the balanc-ing need of each new situation. But remember, you can't restore such "lost" colors unless they are actually present to some degree. Red, for example, usually disappears completely at a depth of thirty feet and there is nothing you can do to restore it. Yellow goes next. This seems to be a pretty conclusive argument in favor of the artificial light proponents for underwater lensmen.

Let's assume we know the location of a sunken wreck. We will set out to photograph it with a simple camera. Should you already own such a beginner's camera but have no case for it, there are novice cases on the market for about seven dollars that consist simply of a glass face plate with a heavy-duty plastic bag attached. You place the camera inside the bag, screw down the watertight metal sealing ring that joins the perimeter of the glass with the

This photo was taken with a medium yellow filter. Note fine detail and good contrast. Without filter, reef would look flat and "burned out."

mouth of the bag, then operate the camera controls by feeling through the soft plastic.

Don't sneer at this. Many a good picture was made in the early days of underwater photography by determined divers who resorted to a surgeon's rubber glove stretched and secured over the glass of an abandoned face mask. Sometimes even a hot water bottle was used! You may like to experiment along these lines with similar materials.

If you own neither camera nor case, you can rent an outfit for a nominal amount at a photographic or sporting goods store, although you will probably have to leave a deposit. Diving centers are your best bet for finding rentable underwater equipment.

Once more as we prepare to leave on a diving trip we check

carefully that your tanks contain sufficient air, that your equipment can pass close scrutiny for damage or improper operation. Incidentally, as soon as we finished using our SCUBA gear for salt water diving in the preceding chapter, we rinsed it thoroughly in fresh water—the mouthpiece and regulator in particular—and dried it before storing. Our camera housing will be given similar care. *Never* allow the camera itself to get wet. Should it become splashed, sponge it off immediately with fresh water. Salt water is insidious; it will enter crevices and eat away from the inside.

The wreck, a small coastal steamer which sprang her old plates and went down in heavy weather, is not far offshore. We select a calm, sunny day and run out to the site in an outboard skiff that affords ample room for divers and their equipment. The outline of the wreck can be seen clearly against the white sand bottom as we anchor nearby and display our diver's flag from the skiff's stern. Ours is by no means the first flag to bob over this easy wreck. It is safe to assume we will find little left of even souvenir value. Yet you experience the rising thrill of adventure as we make final checks of regulators and quick-release harness. There is something fascinating about a wreck.

Before diving we hold the waterproof camera housing just beneath the surface and watch for the bubbles that indicate air leaks. Since the inexpensive plastic box provides only two external controls—shutter release and film advance—we will prefocus the camera for the distance at which we expect to work. Perhaps this beginner's camera has no focusing control; some don't. At any rate, we must preset the shutter speed and lens aperture for what we hope will prove the proper exposure for the film being used.

Down we go, once more kicking from the hips, and this time you swim with arms extended before you, holding the little camera case with both hands. Your air supply gurgles reassuringly in your ears. Once more you are pleasantly surprised at the amount of light beneath the surface. But again it is the strangely pale, dreamlike light which I have cautioned you absorbs bright colors like a Bahama sponge soaks up bilge water.

There are many brilliant colors scattered about the ocean floor below us right now; from yellow and vermilion coral to the vivid orange-brown of a crayfish's spiny back—but our eyes do not record these colors as they really exist. Hence our color camera film can't see them either—unless we employed flash to restore the light balance.

The sunken steamer lies in only thirty feet of water and seems well lighted by this underwater "moonlight." Remember to approach cautiously so you won't be swept against the rusting hull should there be strong currents. Nor will we enter one of the several yawning black companionway doors in the seaweed-grown upper structure. Write it clearly in your SCUBA diver's memory book *never* to enter a wreck at random. Like cave exploration, this is specialized diving which calls for safety lines, standby divers and similar safety precautions.

To insure pictures of best clarity, many underwater photographers strive to focus upon a subject so it is not farther away than

Displaying diver's flag from boat's stern.

one-third their total visibility range. When we reach this distance we stop swimming. A reading of the light meter inside our glass fruit jar confirms that our present camera adjustments will do. I motion for you to take your first picture.

You bring the plastic camera housing up against your face mask to steady it as you sight through the sports finder frame atop the box. The regular camera viewing window cannot be brought close enough to the eye to be used underwater. But you are not satisfied as you prepare to squeeze the release button. At this distance you are too close to the wreck to include the entire hull in the finder. You want to back off to correct this. But I have warned you before our descent that to do this will place additional light scattering and absorbing water particles between subject and camera. If you disregard the one-third-visible-distance rule, you jeopardize picture quality. Once more you begin to appreciate the limitations of underwater photography. So you compromise by snapping several sectional shots of the wreck, including one of the bow with the ship's almost-hidden name.

This is one reason that experienced diving lensmen prefer a wide-angle to a standard lens. Water has the property of bending light rays to decrease your lens' effective angle of vision. Once beneath the surface the working width of a standard lens may be narrowed almost to what you'd have with a telephoto lens on land. And a wide-angle lens, some of which have twice the width of vision of a standard optic, automatically assumes the restricted width of the standard lens you'd use for surface photography.

Another advantage of the wide angle is the deeper zone of sharp focus which it affords—something you should appreciate from our earlier discussion. This means that often you need not take time to refocus to insure a sharp picture of a passing fish or other object.

Of course, should the subject be moving quickly you may need a faster shutter speed to "freeze" its motion. It is a good rule to use the fastest shutter speed possible at all times to safeguard against blur from subject or camera movement. Strive for at least 1/100-second. If film and light conditions permit, higher speeds would be even better. There may be times when you have no choice but to slow down to 1/25 or even less. In such cases a tripod set up against the bottom becomes almost a must. If you

Photographing diver on sunken wreck.

have none, try bracing your body and camera against a rock or other bottom rest. Extra belt weights may help, as can holding on to a line anchored from a surface float. Some professionals drive stakes into the bottom to be gripped or braced against by feet and legs.

With today's wide range of inexpensive still and movie cameras and matching underwater housings, you should experience little difficulty in outfitting yourself with more advanced equipment, if you decide you like SCUBA photography. And you can always economize by buying used equipment, but check it out carefully first.

Most divers prefer the 35mm camera, equipped with a wide-angle lens of 35mm or shorter focal length for "standard" use. The 2¼ by 2¼-inch film size is their second choice, in a reflex housing. The 35mm is small and permits use of a little case that is easily handled and affords the least water resistance. Also, you can fire the 35mm camera thirty-six times before surfacing to reload (as against twelve shots with the 2¼ by 2¼). And this smallest camera affords the best selection of interchangeable lenses and available films.

We have stated how water magnifies all objects so they appear about a third larger than actual size. Perhaps you are wondering how this affects your focusing. A fish, looking larger than it is, actually is farther away than it appears. Forget it. The camera makes the same mistake as your eyes and everything comes out okay.

In movie cameras the 8mm is more popular with sport divers than the 16mm. Both it and the film it uses are the most economical of the two. The same goes for housings. The 16mm does offer better quality and other advantages but these can be disregarded unless you are shooting professionally. Be sure to pan your movie camera slowly and evenly, from a steady stance, just as you would on land. Minimum sequence should be about ten seconds.

An f:1.8 or f:1.9 lens speed is ample for good underwater color movie work. Your still camera lens should be at least f:3.5. Electric-eye cameras have proven valuable where underwater lighting conditions may vary often enough to call for repeated changes.

A good 35mm camera loaded with Plus-X (daylight rating ASA 120) or an equivalent fine-grain black-and-white film can provide you with excellent underwater pictures. The pros sometimes find it necessary to go to the 2¼ by 2¼ and even 4 by 5 film sizes to combat black-and-white grain, but with reasonable care you should get along nicely with Plus-X in 35mm. Tri-X (ASA 400) is almost a must where poor lighting justifies the noticeable grain increase. As for color films, the new Kodachrome II (ASA 25 in daylight) is hard to beat where there is good light. If not, try Anscochrome (ASA 100) or even Super Ektachrome (ASA 160).

Should you try underwater flash, be sure to mount the light "off camera" on an extension arm, or even a separate tripod support. The arm should extend somewhat before the camera and lens, at about a 45-degree angle from vertical. The flash will otherwise strike those water particles immediately before the lens, lighting these up brilliantly as "hot spots" and jeopardizing over-all picture quality.

Example of another type of underwater camera.

To insure handling ease, your underwater camera housing shouldn't be excessively buoyant, lest it affect your own buoyancy. If you "drop" it you might have to chase it back to the surface. Weight it from the inside, if necessary, to achieve neutral buoyancy. Some housings provide an air hose fitting so the case can be pressurized for deep dives. Use caution when pumping air into a case. A hand pump is preferred since excessive pressure may damage both camera and case.

When you return from our wreck-photographing trip and have the film processed and printed you discover that only a few of the pictures turned out the way you'd hoped. The new and strange moonlight in the depths has stolen much of the clarity and impact from the scenes you saw on the ocean's floor. This is why the beginner should experiment first with black-and-white film because purchase cost, processing, and printing expense is considerably less than color.

Nevertheless, you are able to analyze your mistakes—a good sign. Next time you will remember to move in closer, eliminating even more of the light-diffusing water particles between you and subject. You will try to frame fish, interesting coral formations, and similar subjects against plain and contrasting backgrounds to make them stand out better. White sand is always an excellent background for black-and-white photography. You can also benefit by shooting from a low angle so the subject is silhouetted against the surface.

Many SCUBA photographers limit their shooting time to shortly before and after the noon hour when the sun's rays are directly overhead. But you can get interesting front, side, and even backlighting effects when light enters the water at a greater angle. This will, of course, provide less light and call for more exposure. But it can prove well worthwhile.

I promised to show you how to build your own underwater camera housing. We can use the savings from it to buy a new or used 35mm camera of better quality and flexibility than the simple box camera we rented to photograph the sunken steamer.

The housing or case presented here is designed to accommodate such a camera. It is easy to make, costs only about fifteen dollars for materials and operates beautifully.

Assembly Sequence of Case

1. First clamp one end of the ⅜ x 5¾ x 32-inch plastic to the back of the forming block and make the four bends required, Fig. 1. Use a torch to soften the plastic, Figs. 2 and 3, and then press evenly against the point of bend with a wooden block as in Fig. 4.

2. After making the previous bend, the end is overlapped onto the back edge and cemented to it by dipping the joint in a V-shaped tray of methylene chloride. The latter should just cover the joint. When the plastic becomes soft, clamp the joint until the cement sets. Methylene chloride is used for cementing all joints.

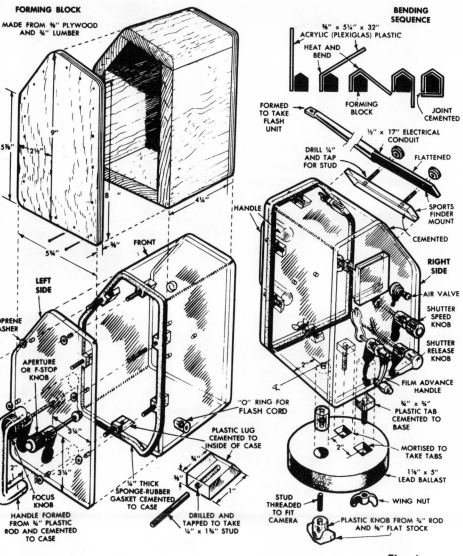

FORMING BLOCK

MADE FROM ⅜" PLYWOOD AND ¾" LUMBER

BENDING SEQUENCE

¾" x 5¼" x 32" ACRYLIC (PLEXIGLAS) PLASTIC

HEAT AND BEND

FORMED TO TAKE FLASH UNIT

FORMING BLOCK

JOINT CEMENTED

½" x 17" ELECTRICAL CONDUIT

FLATTENED

DRILL ¼" AND TAP FOR STUD

SPORTS FINDER MOUNT

CEMENTED

9"

5⅞" 2½"

8"

4¼"

HANDLE

FRONT

5¾" ¾"

LEFT SIDE

RIGHT SIDE

AIR VALVE

SHUTTER SPEED KNOB

SHUTTER RELEASE KNOB

NEOPRENE WASHER

APERTURE OR F-STOP KNOB

"O" RING FOR FLASH CORD

FILM ADVANCE HANDLE

¾" x ¾" PLASTIC TAB CEMENTED TO BASE

3¼"

2" 6

PLASTIC LUG CEMENTED TO INSIDE OF CASE

MORTISED TO TAKE TABS

2" 3¼"

¼" THICK SPONGE-RUBBER GASKET CEMENTED TO CASE

¾"

¾"

1"

2"

1½" x 5" LEAD BALLAST

STUD THREADED TO FIT CAMERA

WING NUT

FOCUS KNOB

DRILLED AND TAPPED TO TAKE ¼" x 1¾" STUD

PLASTIC KNOB FROM ¾" ROD AND ⅜" FLAT STOCK

HANDLE FORMED FROM ¾" PLASTIC ROD AND CEMENTED TO CASE

Fig. 1

3. Sand down edges of plastic on both sides of the case, first smoothing wrinkled corners. Make sure you keep the edges square.

4. Cut out side pieces, check them for tight fit against case edges and cement right side to case. (Cement is poured in shallow stainless or enamel pan to ¼-inch depth, then case is placed in it, right

Fig. 2

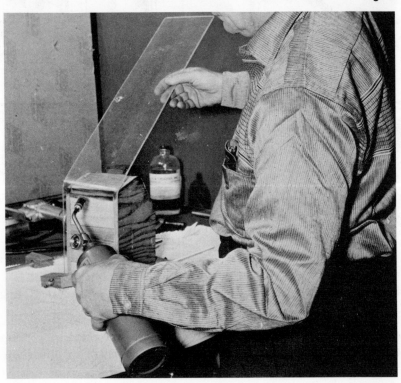

Fig. 3

Fig. 4

side down, Fig. 5. At the same time, cement is brushed on mating surface of side piece.) Clamp until set, Fig. 6. Plastic lugs are made next and cemented to the inside of the case to take the left side, which then is drilled to take the studs as in Fig. 6.

5. Next, the camera is mounted in the case, after drilling a hole in the bottom to take the fastening screw as shown in Fig. 7. The lens board should be fully extended when doing this to assure adequate focusing clearance. Shutter speed and aperture-control

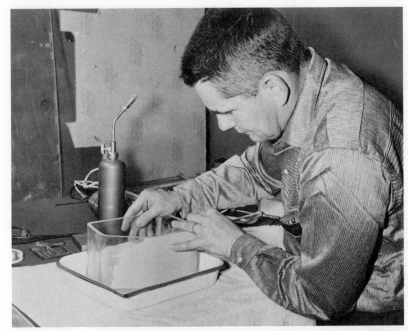

Fig. 5

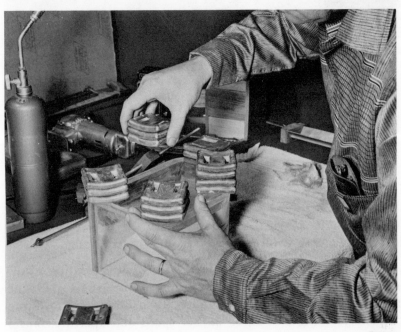

Fig. 6

Fig. 7

shaft holes are located by positioning a spike (large nail) over the centers of these controls on the camera and marking for the hole on the right side first, as in Figs. 8 and 9. A $\frac{1}{4}$-inch hole then is drilled through at the mark, after which the left side is fastened in place temporarily and the same procedure used for marking it to take the aperture-control shaft. The holes to be drilled in the case side for the shutter release, film advance, and focus shafts are best located by first making a template of each side of the camera, with the axial centers of the camera's controls (handle, in case of

Fig. 8

Fig. 9

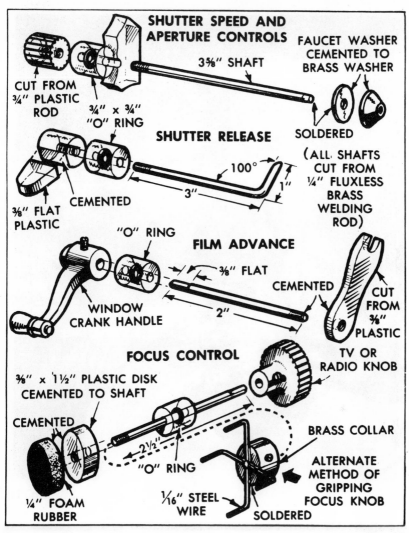

SHUTTER SPEED AND APERTURE CONTROLS

FAUCET WASHER CEMENTED TO BRASS WASHER

3⅝" SHAFT

CUT FROM ¾" PLASTIC ROD

¾" x ¾" "O" RING

SOLDERED

SHUTTER RELEASE

(ALL SHAFTS CUT FROM ¼" FLUXLESS BRASS WELDING ROD)

100°

1"

3"

CEMENTED

⅜" FLAT PLASTIC

"O" RING

FILM ADVANCE

⅜" FLAT

CEMENTED

CUT FROM ⅜" PLASTIC

WINDOW CRANK HANDLE

2"

TV OR RADIO KNOB

FOCUS CONTROL

⅜" x 1½" PLASTIC DISK CEMENTED TO SHAFT

CEMENTED

BRASS COLLAR

2½"

ALTERNATE METHOD OF GRIPPING FOCUS KNOB

"O" RING

¼" FOAM RUBBER

1/16" STEEL WIRE

SOLDERED

Fig. 10

film advance) marked on it. The template then is taped in place on the appropriate case side and the holes drilled as marked.

6. Each control and through-case connection is fitted with an "O"-ring cemented to the outside of the case to seal out water. To assure proper alignment of the O-ring hole with case hole, insert one of the ¼-inch shafts in the latter, then apply methylene chloride to the mating surface and slide the O-ring in place on

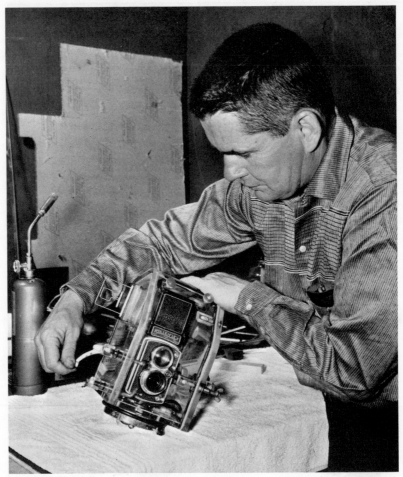

Fig. 11

the shaft. All control assemblies are detailed in Figs. 10 and 11.

7. The air valve is a standard tubeless tire valve, which is installed on the case with the parts that come with it. Air pressure from a few pumps of a tire pump before each submersion will leave a trail of bubbles in the event of a leak and give you time to surface before water enters.

8. The lead ballast at the bottom of the case (see Fig. 1) is necessary to counteract the buoyant effect of the entrapped air in it. About eight pounds of lead are required (enough to allow the camera and case to settle slowly in the water) so that it won't float away when you set it down. A one-pound coffee can makes an excellent form for casting the lead weight.

9. When forming the handle from plastic rod, be sure to apply heat entirely around the point of bend. The $\frac{1}{4}$-inch sponge-rubber gasket (see Fig. 1) that seals the removable side of the case is cut in one piece from a bathroom mat and cemented in place with electrical coating dope, such as Scotchkote. The thick part of a truck inner tube also may be used for gasket material.

Acrylic plastic scratches easily, so when making the case and later when transporting or storing it, protect the surface with a soft cloth. Shallow scratches can be removed by buffing with Cadillac polishing compound or similar fine-grade buffing material.

6. Spear Fishing

Spear fishing in some areas has become a controversial subject because a minority group of inconsiderate divers have abused the sport. A large portion of the fish-filled Florida Keys, for example, is closed to the use of spearguns as an underwater preserve.

I once saw a burly SCUBA diver return to dock with his outboard boat heaped high with choice gray snapper. There were so many speared fish in that skiff that I knew he could never eat them all—nor even clean them in time to give them away.

"Why?" I asked him. "Why so many? You must have wiped out an entire hole. Why spoil the sport for the rest of us?" He became quite abusive at that.

Spear fishing is officially recognized as an international competitive sport. It will remain the fine sport that it is only if divers remember to be good sportsmen. The Underwater Society of America urges you to waste no living thing, pointing out that man is only the temporary custodian of the wildlife resource that must be maintained on a renewable basis, shared by the line fisherman, the commercial fisherman and the skin diver.

To be a good sportsman, the diver must be something more than a conservationist, too. Obey existing laws. Don't trespass or leave a littered beach behind you. Don't annoy rod and reel fishermen, rob the commercial man's lobster pots, and so on. Don't work too close to swimmers and worry them over a dangerous spear sent carelessly in their direction. Don't impede boat traffic needlessly with your floating diver's flag when you are not actually diving.

We've pointed out that small marine plants and animals congregate where bottom obstructions offer protection against sweeping currents. Hence fish are attracted to these natural feeding stations.

So look for rocks, bottom crevices, wrecks, and similar inviting spots when you set out to spear fish. A reef drop-off or a rock jetty is usually a good place to hunt if fish are in the vicinity. They like to follow such natural barriers while searching for food. And there are handy holes and cracks for hiding from danger. When you hunt, swim with the current as the fish do. This saves your strength. Or take up a position along a swimway and wait for the current to carry the fish to you.

Practically all sincere spear fishermen frown upon the use of SCUBA while enjoying their sport. They work with the snorkel only. SCUBA is hardly sporting—unless you must go really deep to engage some particularly difficult quarry. Remember how the fish showed little fear of us during our dives to explore and photograph? The same unfair advantage would exist were you to spear fish with SCUBA. They might at times flee into hiding places as you approached, but if you waited a few minutes they'd soon swim out again to accept you as one of them. You can't miss under such conditions. So for our underwater fishing trip we will content ourselves with the simple snorkeling equipment you began with—plus a speargun of your choice.

Your "gun" can vary from a simple hand lance or a spear powered by a looped rubber sling at one end, used much like a slingshot, to the more powerful multiple rubber-, spring-, air-, and gas-powered guns. For big fish with tough hides, and for large open hunting areas where a shaft must travel farther, you will need a stronger speargun, and vice versa. Many underwater anglers, like their "light tackle" counterparts above the surface, prefer to pursue only small fish, using a simple low-powered gun. These sportsmen claim, and probably rightly, that their brand of fishing offers just as much satisfaction as killing a 300-pound jewfish with a heavy CO_2 weapon.

Some skin divers, in fact, refuse to use anything but a simple hand spear, powered only by the diver's arm. This is the only type of shaft permitted in some waters, and you may be surprised how good you can become with it if you have the time and patience. Be sure to check what legal restrictions may exist in the area where you intend to spear fish. Some states prohibit use of certain of the stronger spearguns and usually all guns are forbidden in fresh waters. The authorities you consult can also prove

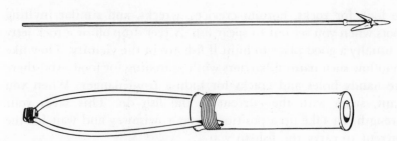

Simple speargun powered by a looped rubber sling much like a slingshot.

helpful in providing pamphlets describing the native fish, their locations and habits, as well as other useful information. So can local divers and sport shops. It may not be safe, for example, to eat the oysters and clams you may find in some waters.

You will promptly discover that without the advantage of SCUBA you must really match wits with the fish to get within shooting range, usually six to fifteen feet. Try to dive quietly from the surface, without splashing, and when you approach the quarry, swim without unnecessary body movement. Make sure not to bump bottom growths, or let your lance strike a rock, since this sets up vibrations in the water that alarm the fish. Take your time.

This, of course, is not easy. Time has once more become quite important. You can hold your breath for only a short while before you must resurface. And when you return, the fish may be gone. This, then, is where the sport comes in. Aha! There is a good-sized fish right ahead. Can you see him peeking at you from behind that clump of undulating bottom grass?

But what's this? Our finned observer who would likely have remained right there had you been carrying only a camera now moves off. What's more, he seems to persist in remaining just out of range.

We stop. He stops. We swim ahead. He retreats. Obviously, he is enjoying this playful game of stop and go. But you are not. In fact, it soon becomes quite exasperating.

Finally he stops in the shadow of a big grass-grown bottom rock to turn and regard you owlishly from protruding eyes that do not wink. You pause. Is this some new kind of trick he's making ready to pull? Or is he silly enough to believe you can't see him quietly

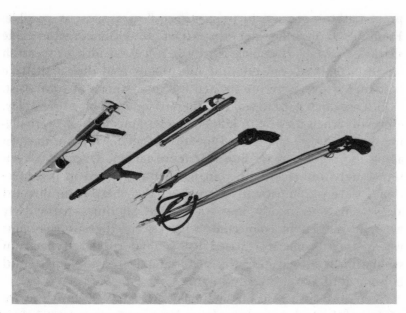

More powerful multiple rubber-, spring-, air-, and gas-powered guns.

finning there in the shadows through your fancy new wide-vision face mask? You ease closer. You've learned that the trick is to approach gently, making as few extra motions as possible. Fish feel these disturbances.

You can see your target's gills moving; you are now that close. You get ready to shoot. The rubber sling is carefully looped over the thumb and first finger of one hand, then stretched with the other hand. It's much like bow and arrow shooting. You aim carefully for a head or spine shot since this will immediately paralyze and it is tiring work to chase a wounded fish. Then you fire. The shaft strikes just aft of the gills, a good shot, and the spearhead buries itself.

The fish tries to dart away, but it cannot. The movable wings of the sharp barb splay outward, holding it fast to the lance with a short metal cable. The lance meanwhile has come loose from its detachable head at the fish's first tug and you are holding fast to it by means of its rubber sling. Feel how the fish struggles! Had it been a larger specimen you wonder if you could have held it. But soon the struggles cease. You've speared your first fish.

Next step is to get the bleeding specimen into boat or leakproof washtub secured to your surface float as soon as possible. Fresh blood in the water can attract unwelcome visitors, like sharks or barracuda—which is why it is a good idea to spearfish on an incoming ocean tide; the fish usually feed then and strike best anyway. *Never* secure speared fish to a stringer at your waist.

Fish are often hard to see from the surface, even on a bright day, especially when they lie in holes or under grass beds or overhanging shelves. So we take a good breath and go down again to swim along the bottom as we hunt for more targets. Once when you forget and swim close with your handspear pointed in my direction, I wave you impatiently away. Keep that sharp point directed away from your buddy, and yourself, at all times—particularly when it is used in connection with one of the stronger guns which are customarily carried loaded and cocked. When you swim with a cocked gun, the shaft should always point toward bottom until you are ready to aim.

Never load such guns on land, or in a boat. Wait until you are ready to fish. And even then always be sure of your target before firing, especially if the water is dirty or the light poor. Divers have been killed by the speargun shafts of friends—mistaken for fish in bad visibility.

Spearheads are dangerously sharp and can cause trouble sometimes even without being fired. Last year a friend—an experienced spear fisherman—made the mistake of letting such a barb ruin his surface float even before he could make his first dive. He'd walked into the surf backward in the approved manner, towing the float behind him into the breakers. But he'd forgotten to tie his speargun securely to the float and a striking comber dislodged it, causing the sharp barb to slice through the rubber.

On the bottom again, you are suddenly confronted with a wall of living silver. A school of choice Spanish mackerel has moved in. These tempting targets always provide keen sport. But before you can recover and get your handspear cocked the fish are gone again.

We come now to a rocky area. After swimming over it for only a few yards, I stop you. I make a thumb-down motion with one hand, the standard skin divers' signal to direct your attention bottomward. You look and can see nothing unusual. This worries you. Is it a shark or barracuda? Not at all. It's a colony of hidden lobsters. Soon you, too, become aware of their characteristic raspy scrapings ("like tin cans"). These may be caused by moving the feelers together; I'm not sure.

"Now we will have some real sport," I promise gleefully as we surface to substitute handspear for heavy canvas work gloves. "Remember that the best way to grab one of these bugs is from behind the head. If you must approach from the front, try to wrap your fingers around the horns, which are at the base of the feelers."

These are spiny crayfish of the type found in Florida, Mexico and California waters. They do not have pincers like the Maine lobster of the northeastern U.S. coast.

Down we go, homing on the odd sounds which now appear to be coming from beneath a long rocky ledge. As we arrive at the ledge and grip it to lower ourselves underneath, there is a flurry of motion. We see several of the bugs scuttle for cover. One big fellow nearest you struggles mightily as you grasp it by the legs. This is a mistake. Two of the legs immediately break off, and the bug escapes.

You grab another of the spiny crustaceans by the tail just as it tries to disappear into a rocky hole—and this proves to be another mistake. For the powerful tail instantly whips closed into a tight arc about your hand. You feel the sharp pain of fingers being crushed despite the protective glove. I join the struggle, however, and we soon wrest your hand free.

The remaining lobsters have escaped to the safety of holes and crevices. Here and there pairs of long feelers protrude watchfully, but these duck quickly from sight—or break off—the moment you touch them. So we return to the surface, carrying our prizes tail-up on their backs, for deposit in the game sack on our float.

As your underwater experience increases, you will learn to recognize the lobster, fish, and other sounds. The grouper is probably the loudest "talker" of all. This fish is also one of the dumbest of all. It will, for example, try to swim back into the same hole where you first shot it and dragged it into the ocean.

Don't make the mistake of fastening speargun or shaft line to your body, regardless what kind of fish you pursue. One amateur South American diver did this and the large grouper he shot, with too-light equipment, proved too much to handle.

Unable to let go, the novice pushed the panic button. He forgot to use his knife on the taut nylon which was pulling him into the depths behind the wounded fish. His buddies managed to rescue him, but not before he reached a depth where the pressure was dangerous. He was lucky.

Keep in mind, when grabbing for lobsters or crabs, or while searching for clams or oysters or other shellfish, never to reach into areas you can't examine first. Moray eels like to hide in such places, as may some of the few other unfriendly types.

Most feared of the unfriendly ones, of course, is the shark. Much heated discussion has taken place over the years whether these brutes will or will not deliberately attack a diver. In this connection, I have interviewed dozens of shark authorities, including the veteran handliner who started the first U.S. commercial shark oil and hide fishery. The general opinion of such experts is simply, "No one can predict just what a shark will do. Why take a chance by putting yourself in a vulnerable position?"

This should be the spear fisherman's attitude, too. Most sharks, like barracuda and other fish, will regard you curiously, then proceed on their way. A shark will continue to move restlessly in your presence simply because it has no swim bladder and would sink otherwise. However, if it should appear more interested than that—if, for example, it begins to circle you—then seek the safety of boat or shore at once. But do this without giving the impression you are running away; swim with measured, even strokes. Back away slowly first, if necessary, before you turn tail. Fish seem to depend upon water vibrations to indicate the vulnerability of a potential victim. A barracuda, for instance, a basically curious and cowardly fish, may ignore a smaller specimen—then attack it greedily moments later when the smaller fish takes a baited hook and begins to struggle.

Never molest any shark, regardless how small. To injure it may quickly attract larger sharks. Never swim where sharks are known to be, and always avoid murky or night water which prevents you from observing approaching fish, and them from seeing you clearly.

A concluding word of caution. Spear fishing, like diving itself, can mean many things to many people. For the Pacific Coast diver it may mean happy hours spent prying up abalone with a tire iron.

Never molest any shark!

For the Floridian or Bahamian it may mean diving for conchs or stalking any of their 600 different varieties of sub-tropic fish. Wherever you may dive, however, or whatever may be your choice of underwater diversion, always remember that you are out of your natural element—and be cautious.

Always keep your head. It is very easy to lose track of time in this fascinating new world, for example, so that you unconsciously use up your strength and may find yourself too weak to cope with a big fish when you spear one, or to make it back to shore as the sun sets. Enjoy yourself to the fullest, yes, but remain constantly alert to your surroundings and aware of your own limitations. Take no chances. Live to dive on another day in this new-found freedom.

A good innertube can be converted to provide long service as a sturdy surface float to support not only your diver's flag but game sack, basket or metal fish tub in its center. It need not be a large bus-type tube since this only makes it harder to tow while swimming.

Wrap stout cord about the tube to provide convenient hand grips when clinging to the float to rest. These wraps will also serve as convenient sack, basket or tub anchoring points around the tube's inner perimeter. Some divers prefer to sew two gunny sacks together to make a bag about one and one-half times the standard length. This permits the user to swing the bag's closed end up onto the float ring while underway, thereby reducing surface drag while towing.

A bag or net used thus will not, of course, prevent blood from freshly speared fish from entering the water. So when spear fishing, substitute the gunny sack with a small circular galvanized wash tub, tying this in position inside the tube just as the mouth of the sack or net was tied.

7. Advice from the Experts

Zale Parry, the attractive California housewife who holds the women's world record for deep diving, urges you not to indulge in indiscriminate SCUBA diving in the hope of establishing an endurance record of any kind.

"It is my belief that deep diving should be accomplished by only the skilled who have been trained and who are compelled because of duty to dive deep in order to enhance the knowledge of this last frontier," she told the writer.

"The two deep dives that I have made—209 feet in the open sea and 307 feet in a decompression chamber—were controlled experiments conducted by engineers and scientists who paid strict adherence to all laws of deep diving while the tests were conducted. I have no intention of making more deep dives. In fact, I find my greatest fun in the sunlit shallows where my underwater camera can record the lively beauty."

Mrs. Parry lives in Los Angeles where she is associated with Scientific Underwater Research Enterprises. As might be expected, she has had many exciting diving experiences. However, the incident which stands out in her memory as the most frightening took place, strangely, on the *surface*.

"I was only about two blocks offshore in the Gulf of California one sunny day, swimming in on a surfmat with a roosterfish I'd speared, when a large pelican suddenly appeared from nowhere overhead and dive-bombed into the waves uncomfortably close to me. The belligerent bird did this over and over, seeming to come closer each time, until my blood pressure began to soar nervously.

"I was certain he was after me—until I noticed that his bill was pitifully broken. Perhaps this deformity had rendered my attacker helpless in finding food in the usual manner. At any rate, he was definitely after the wounded roosterfish on my surfmat— or me, too—and I was glad when I made it safely back to shore."

Newton A. Perry of Ocala, Florida, was once described by sports-caster Grantland Rice as the best all-around swimmer in America. Speaking of the many and unusual underwater routines "The Human Fish" had perfected for presentation on film and in person to an appreciative public, Rice told Newt Perry, "We consider you the father of underwater swimming in its highly developed form."

During the past thirty years, this veteran has taught over twelve thousand persons swimming, lifesaving, skin and SCUBA diving. Today he and his wife Dot (one-time U.S. team diving trainee whom Perry met through Olympics diving-swimming champion Katherine Rawls) jointly operate a swimming school, serving as their own instructors (over eight hundred students enrolled at the year of this writing). And today, as always, Newt Perry finds physi-cal fitness and a willingness to learn the two main steps toward swimming and diving success.

"I cannot overemphasize the importance of being in top physi-cal condition at all times," he says. "You hear constantly of acci-dents that result from panic. Yet the beginner must not only know what to do to combat panic; he must also be in physical condition to carry out what he's been taught.

"I've never lost a student from accident, because it is a standard requirement of mine that he pass the regular course in lifesaving and learn all he possibly can about swimming before I agree to teach him SCUBA diving."

Perry believes it is criminal to sell youngsters and adults diving equipment without positive proof the purchaser is qualified to use such equipment.

As proof of what he means by a beginner's physical fitness and willingness to learn, The Human Fish cites an experience, one of many he's had while working with motion-picture companies. His services were engaged to teach star Ann Blyth to swim in just ten days so she could perform in the movie "Mr. Peabody and the Mermaid."

"At the outset I felt I'd been given an impossible job—but then I didn't know the good physical condition and sheer determination of Miss Blyth," recalls Perry. "Not only did I teach her to swim, she also learned how to wear a 30-pound mermaid's tail and propel herself through the water with it.

"And, if that doesn't seem next to impossible, let me tell you what else I was required to teach her. One sequence in the film called for her to swim down to an underwater castle. There a large conch shell afforded an underwater air-trap where she could breathe—if she could find an opening which was just large enough to permit entry of her head and shoulders! She was not allowed to carry any air with her or use a face mask, of course.

"Ann had a real hard time. It was difficult for her to get down the twenty feet to the bottom and adjust herself to the water pressure there—just as it is difficult for any beginner. She was willing to learn, however. And after we'd practiced the dive at least fifty times she learned how to do it.

"I still find it difficult to believe this student started as a rank beginner and ten days later was swimming and diving like an expert—but Ann Blyth had what it took to meet the challenge."

Graceful Patsie Boyett, one of the world's outstanding female swimmers and divers, echoes Newton Perry's timely advice and adds one important suggestion.

"I would like to give this motto to all beginning divers; simply this, and in this order: good health, good instruction and *good common sense!*" says charming Patsie who is a pioneer in underwater hose breathing and who has swum for personalities like Arthur Godfrey, Billy Rose, Esther Williams, John Payne, and Terry Moore, to name a few.

She is quick to cite three examples during the long years of her experience where she failed to use good common sense herself and suffered near-disaster as a result. Each came as a result of trying to overdo while in the water; a common mistake of the beginner.

"The first time, I passed out from swimming too long during early pregnancy," she admits. "Next I foolishly tried to push myself too far while trying to break a breath control record. The third time I was performing live before a nation-wide TV audience.

"In the last example I was featured in an underwater ballet. Because I was wearing an ungainly ballet costume, complete with tiara, it would take me at least two minutes to dive from the surface, without the use of mask or fins, find a clear plastic air hose to take a deep breath from on the bottom, turn off the hose and face the camera.

"However, when it came time for the show to begin—and remember that this was a live show; there could be no retakes— we discovered that the plastic air hose, which was purposely of the clear type so the audience couldn't see it in the water, was also invisible to *me*. I couldn't find it, hard as I tried.

"My cue was coming up fast. Already there was too little time left for me to get down to the bottom comfortably, as we'd rehearsed. Fifteen girl divers were scheduled to hit the water's surface at any moment. However, just as I decided to withdraw my act from the program a girl friend in a following act found my air hose.

"On impulse I decided to go on. Somehow I got down and into position in forty-five seconds—leaving less than five seconds to prepare myself for the camera—and went through the entire routine. I lost consciousness on the way back to shore. Fortunately, someone was handy to grab me—just like the other two times."

Diminutive Patsie often has the satisfaction of playing the role of off-camera underwater "safety man" to handsome movie heroes who swim before the cameras while females swoon in the audience. "And, girls, if they depend upon *me* to keep them from drowning that makes them even braver than you thought!" she says modestly.

Her funniest diving experience stems from just such a situation. On location with a Hollywood movie crew, Patsie was hovering watchfully in the depths, acting as safety for husky Ricou Browning while he worked as "The Creature of the Black Lagoon."

Browning, long-time friend of Patsie and her husband, Bud (she includes both men in her list of top American male divers), had to depend entirely upon her for air. At regular intervals, she would swim to him, carrying a small hose on-camera since he was dressed in a grotesque alligator-skin-like costume, the large claws of which made it impossible to hold the tiny air hose to his mouth.

Patsie and Browning had an understanding that should she ever manage to count to ninety between such breathing pauses something would be wrong and she must bring the hose at once, even if this meant interrupting the filming. And that's just what happened.

"I guess it just about fractured the cameramen, too," she says with a grin. "They were in the midst of a grim, dramatic scene in the shadowy depths wherein three vengeful SCUBA divers carrying deadly weapons and explosives were searching this underwater cavern for the hideous Creature of the Black Lagoon. And there I come swimming suddenly into view: a small girl in a two-piece bathing suit. I catch the Creature neatly from behind, jerk his frightening head mask around and shove an air hose into his mouth. Then, holding him fearlessly about the waist, I swim off with him . . . out of the scene."

Pioneer SCUBA man Glen Galvin, who was skin diving nearly thirty years ago with South Sea bamboo goggles and, later, with the early Japanese face plates, relates this grim personal experience as proof that a shark's actions should always be considered unpredictable:

"Hollywood cameraman Lamar Boren, the two Rickter brothers and I were diving at Cocos Island, off the west coast of South America. We were filming some scenes for the Warner Bros. picture 'The Old Man and the Sea' showing hungry sharks tearing to pieces a large marlin alongside a small skiff at the surface.

"To do this we had to shoot upward and for protection we had placed Lamar inside an 8-foot steel cage, completely open at the front so he could make pictures. A man stood guard on either side of him, armed with a blunt spear to ward off the sharks if necessary. I stood in the back, working the up and down button, holding the still camera—and praying. The cage resembled a jail cell and, we were to discover, it could have become somebody's tomb.

"The cage was suspended about twenty feet below the surface from a boom on a tuna boat. The doomed marlin and the small boat were about fifteen feet from us. We had been making pictures like this for eleven days and this was the last marlin we had.

"Suddenly one of the hungry sharks tore off a chunk of meat and headed right into our cage. The guard at Boren's right elbow jabbed at this fish but it was already so close that Lamar joined in, swinging his camera at it. The grip's spear succeeded in deflecting the shark's path so that it passed us close on the outside of the cage. But the force of the cameraman's swing had upset both him and the guard, causing them to fall down in a corner.

"This left the whole front of the cage unprotected, since the second guard had stepped out of the way and now stood at the rear, alongside me. And so another shark came right in on us. There was no time for the guard to use his spear.

"Without hesitating, he placed his hand against the big fish's head and pushed hard. The man-eater performed a sudden U-turn and flipped out of the cage just as we broke through the surface— I had long ago pressed the 'up' button, believe me!"

Index

Index

About the Author

GEORGE X. SAND was born in Manahawkin, New Jersey, on April 16, 1915. He attended public schools in New Jersey, the Massachusetts Radio and Telegraph School in Boston, and the Capitol Radio Engineering Institute in Washington, D. C. Now a freelance magazine writer and photojournalist, he is a director of the Outdoor Writers Association of America. He has had hundreds of articles, fiction features, and photo stories published in top U.S. magazines. He has also written short stories that have been reprinted a dozen times, used in English books, and used by the State Department for broadcast into Iron Curtain countries.

Mr. Sand says this of his career as a free lancer: "Looking back, it's been a wild, wonderful hodgepodge of victories and defeats, of shrieks and sighs. I've traveled over a million miles—by plane, bus, car, jeep, horse and dugout canoe. At my age now, I doubt that I'd do it over. And yet, there's nothing I'd rather do. I love adventure."

His greatest love is the outdoors, particularly the deep, remote forests and other areas, and he is happiest when he can go there to camp, hunt, and fish. He is very familiar with the sport of skin diving and has many friends among the best-known skin divers today.

George Sand, his wife, and their two teenage daughters live in Boca Raton, Florida.

A HAWTHORN BOOK

Skin and Scuba Diving was designed by Sue Crooks and was set in type by Harry Sweetman Typesetting Corp. of New York City. Presswork was done by Universal Lithographers, Inc., and binding was done by Montauk Book Manufacturing Co., Inc. The body type was set on the Linotype in Baskerville, a modern reproduction of the types cut in 1760 by John Baskerville, of Birmingham, England, reflecting the style of stone inscriptions.

Action Books For Today's Young Adults

Here is a new series of hobby books produced in association with *Popular Mechanics Magazine,* specialists in this field of activity and information. The subjects of these books have been carefully selected from lists submitted to librarians throughout the country and from *Popular Mechanics'* reader response to their magazine, to meet the needs of today's hobby enthusiast. Written and checked by experts in their subjects and profusely illustrated with photographs and line drawings, Action Books will provide a fresh and modern approach to the hobby field.

From rock collecting and skin diving to archaeology and forestry this new series will include a wide range of subjects that will offer variety, activity and knowledge. Although primarily designed for those who have already begun their study and investigation into their favorite hobby, Action Books will also be useful to the beginner. Each book will give the fullest details possible on its subject. They are handbooks and field guides that may be used while in the process of experimentation. They are, as well, dictionaries that will make the specialized terms, charts, tables, and sources of the most useful equipment clear and easy to find.

Action Books For Today's Young Adults is an unusual and outstanding series. These books will not only be fascinating to read but will also provide a complete, helpful and useful guide to all those who find pride and enjoyment in making their hobby an accomplishment of real merit.